✛ ✛ ✛ ✛ ✛ ✛ ✛ ✛ ✛

TEEN
People
OF THE BIBLE

✛ ✛ ✛ ✛ ✛ ✛ ✛ ✛ ✛

TEEN People OF THE BIBLE

Celebrity Profiles
of Real Faith and Tragic Failure

Daniel Darling

NEW HOPE
PUBLISHERS

Birmingham, Alabama

New Hope® Publishers
P. O. Box 12065
Birmingham, AL 35202-2065
www.newhopepublishers.com

New Hope® Publishers is a division of WMU®.

Library of Congress Cataloging-in-Publication Data
Darling, Daniel, 1978-
  Teen people of the Bible : celebrity profiles of real faith and tragic failure / by Daniel Darling.
  p. cm.
  ISBN 978-1-59669-088-2 (sc)
  1. Christian teenagers—Religious life. 2. Bible—Biography. I. Title.
BV4531.3.D37 2007
242'.63—dc22
    2007016927

All Scripture quotations, unless otherwise indicated, are taken from The Holy Bible, King James Version.

Scripture quotations marked (NKJV) are taken from the New King James Version. Copyright © 1982 by Thomas Nelson, Inc. Used by permission. All rights reserved.

Scripture quotations marked (NIV) are taken from the HOLY BIBLE, NEW INTERNATIONAL VERSION®. NIV®. Copyright ©1973, 1978, 1984 by International Bible Society. Used by permission of Zondervan. All rights reserved.

Scripture quotations marked (NASB) are taken from the New American Standard Bible®. Copyright © 1960, 1962, 1963, 1968, 1971, 1972, 1973, 1975, 1977, 1995 by The Lockman Foundation. Used by permission.

Scripture quotations marked (*The Message*) are taken from *The Message* by Eugene H. Peterson. Copyright © 1993, 1994, 1995, 1996, 2000, 2001, 2002. Used by permission of NavPress Publishing Group.

ISBN-10: 1-59669-088-7
ISBN-13: 978-1-59669-088-2

N076125 • 0508 • 1M2

Table of Contents

✛ ✛ ✛ ✛ ✛ ✛ ✛ ✛ ✛ ✛ ✛ ✛ ✛ ✛ ✛ ✛ ✛

Acknowledgments

Writing a book is a collective effort, so it would be a shame not to mention the many people whose hard work and influence brought me to this place.

First, I have to thank my beautiful wife, Angela, who endured many late nights and Saturdays with me staring into the screen of my laptop. Without her patience and her belief in my dreams, I never would have completed this book. She's more than a wife; she's also a best friend and soul mate.

Second, I must mention my parents who gave me the privilege of growing up in a Christian home and fostered an environment where I could best pursue a relationship with God. It has always been Mom and Dad who said, "You're going to be an author someday" (even after I'd written an awful book report in fourth grade!).

I also must thank Julie Dearyan, who has been my boss, writing mentor, and coach for almost a decade. She gave me a job and a chance when I was just a green-behind-the-ears college student. Along the way, she has helped to nurture the gift God has put in my heart. Julie and her husband, Neal, are some of our dearest friends and ministry partners.

I also want to thank the rest of the Victory In Grace team, who gave me such great encouragement throughout this process. I love working with them in bringing the gospel to people around the world through a variety of new and creative media. I want to specifically thank Cameron Edwards, my trustworthy assistant, who has been an invaluable asset in the creation of this book.

James A. Scudder, my pastor and mentor, has always believed in me and has given me opportunities to succeed. His clear teaching and gentle wisdom have shaped much of my life. I'm forever in his debt.

Of course, this book wouldn't be a book without Andrea Mullins at New Hope Publishers. From the very beginning, she saw potential in this idea of a student devotional book focusing on teens in the Bible. Every step of the way, she championed this idea. I'll never forget the opportunity she gave this first-time author.

I also must give credit to many others. The teens at Quentin Road Bible Baptist Church gave me advice on what teens are really looking for in a devotional. Several seasoned experts—Jesse Florea, Kyle Duncan, Suzie Eller, and Sarah Bragg—shared great wisdom on writing for teens. Elizabeth and Jim George, dear friends, put their reputation on the line to endorse my project. Thank you.

I'm also grateful to authors Jackie Kendall, Charles Stone, and Stephen and Janet Bly for their early endorsements. And my writer's critique group, which includes Maureen Lang, Suzanne Slade, Dawn Hill, Julie Dahlberg, Joanna Bradford, and Sherri Gallagher, has sharpened my words and cheered me every step of the way.

Lastly, it has been a real pleasure to work with Joyce Dinkins and Tina Atchenson in shaping this book and bringing it to the widest possible teen audience. God bless you and the work you do with New Hope Publishers.

Introduction

Jesus often spoke in parables. When He came to this earth and spoke to the multitudes, He seldom just preached. Oh, preaching has its place, of course, but in the course of every sermon, He told a story. He shared illustrations from the lives of farmers and ranchers; businessmen and fishermen; warriors and kings. Each had a kernel of truth that could change the way those people lived.

When I was young, I remember how intimidating it was to pick up a Bible and begin to read it. I knew that daily Bible study was important if I really wanted to get to know the Lord, but honestly, I thought it was hard to make it relate to my everyday life.

What could I learn from the biblical figures of 2,000 years ago? These men and women seemed mythical giants, larger-than-life superstars. Did they face any of the temptations I face on a daily basis? Were they gifted with a spiritual gene that helped them "automatically" follow God?

As I got older, I began to realize that men and women of the Scriptures were people like you and me. They were people who failed miserably at times. They were men who forsook their mission and women who doubted God. Their stories are far more gripping than any fictional work you will ever read.

Jesus said that the stories in the Scriptures were included so you and I could get to know Him better (John 5:39). That's my objective with this book—to help you get to know God in a more personal way by digging deep into the personal lives of young people in the Scriptures who chose to follow Him.

What's encouraging is that their stories are not made-for-TV movies. They don't often have Hollywood-type endings. You'll see that those heroes and heroines you've learned about in Sunday School were not perfect. They didn't always do the right thing. Most importantly, they were people like you. While their lives were dramatically different in terms of culture, they, too, faced many issues you face.

I also don't want to imply that I've found all the answers to life's questions, because I haven't. But I know a God who does have the answers. Not only is He interested in your life, but He also wants you to know Him in a personal way and wants to use you to accomplish great things—things you couldn't even dream of if you tried.

If that's your aim, I hope you'll enjoy this journey. Along the way, you'll have some fun, share some laughs, and hopefully pick up some important life principles that can help you boldly live out your faith.

How to Use This Book

1. **Use it with your Bible, not to replace your Bible.** The purpose of *Teen People of the Bible* is to jump-start your walk with God by bringing a fresh perspective on some of the teen characters in the Bible. Keep your Bible open to the Storyline verses as you read each day in the Digging Deeper section.

2. **Take the 100-day challenge.** Challenge yourself to stay in the Word for 100 days. Reward yourself with a new book or CD after 100 days if you make the goal. You'll be surprised how your life will change after only 100 days of spending time in God's Word.

3. **Meditate on the Action Verse each day.** Ask God to show you what that verse means to your life. Write the verse on a note card or put it on your computer screen saver. If you really want a challenge, memorize the verse and recite it to a friend or family member.

4. **Put yourself in the shoes of the teen you read about each day.** Picture yourself swapping lives with that teen. What would you do in his or her situation? What would he or she do in your situation?

5. **Take time to journal your thoughts and pray to God.** Be honest with God about what you are experiencing. Let Him know how you feel about people, issues, and things that bother you. Ask Him for grace and wisdom in making decisions.

6. **Take a look back.** After you've been reading *Teen People of the Bible* for a few days or weeks, review some of your earliest journal entries. Did God answer your prayers? What has changed in your life since then? How has your attitude changed? What have you learned?

A Quick Word About Salvation

This book is written to those who know Jesus and those who want to know Him. But if you're not there yet, if you are not a Christian, please don't throw it down in disappointment. It's for you too. All I ask is that you sneak ahead to the back of the book to a section entitled, "How to Know for Sure You Are Going to Heaven." Until you become a child of God, you cannot really know God. You don't have the security of knowing where you will spend your eternity. When you do trust Him, let me be the first to welcome you to the family of God.

—Dan Darling

DAY 1

How can I get to heaven?

Today's Teen: Cain
Today's Action Verse: Hebrews 12:24
Storyline: Genesis 3:1 through 4:5

Cain Speaks Today: *"God's favor isn't based on our good works, but is based on His grace."*

Digging Deeper: What was the big deal about Cain's sacrifice? Wasn't he trying to do a good thing by bringing the very best from his fields, groves, and orchards? Well, when you understand God's purpose in the sacrifices, you'll see why what Cain did was so wrong.

Sacrifices were more than ancient rituals. When Adam and Eve fell (disobeyed God) in the Garden of Eden, God sacrificed an animal to provide coverings for Adam and Eve. In the Old Testament, God required animal sacrifices as atonement for sins. Abraham sacrificed a lamb God provided (Genesis 22:7–8, 13). God through Moses commanded each Israelite house-hold to sacrifice a perfect lamb as the Lord's passover (Exodus 12:3–4, 11). These lambs were symbolic of the Messiah, who would later come to be a sacrifice for the sins of all mankind.

So when Cain offered the fruits of the ground, it was a slap in the face to God. It was as though he was telling God, "I don't need your sacrifice—I can do it myself." People have the same reaction to Jesus today. They look at His sacrifice on the cross that provides the free gift of salvation and say, "Nah, I think I'll try to work my way to heaven. I'll try to be good." But even the works of the greatest person in the world are not good enough to cover his or her sins.

Just Like You: Jeremy grew up in a church-going family. It's not like he hated it—he made some good friends in the youth group, kind of liked the pastor, and thought that Christianity was a pretty good way to live his life. But after a while, Jeremy started resenting religion because he just didn't feel he was good enough to make God happy.

He tried really hard not to sin. He tried to control his thoughts. He tried to hang with pretty good guys at school. And he strived to help people he thought were in need. But he couldn't be perfect. Just when he thought he had this sin thing worked out, he'd mess up.

Maybe I just don't have what it takes, Jeremy said to himself. So he gave up and started living anyway he wanted.

One day a friend invited Jeremy to a two-day youth camp. He didn't want to go, but his friend told him that there would be a lot of fun activities like fishing, basketball, and hiking.

On the first night, one of the leaders shared the gospel, and Jeremy learned for the very first time that salvation is *free*—all he had to do was believe. He had never heard this before. Later that night, he found his Bible and reread the verses the youth leader shared earlier (Ephesians 2:8–9; John 1:12; Acts 16:31). It made so much sense. Jeremy realized he didn't need to perform to make God happy; believing and receiving the gift of Christ's finished work at Calvary were enough.

Did You Know? In the Old Testament, God sometimes signaled His acceptance of a sacrifice with fire from heaven, which came and consumed it (1 Kings 18:36–39; 1 Chronicles 21:26; 2 Chronicles 7:1).

Today's Prayer: *Jesus, I know I can't work my way to heaven. I believe that You died to pay for my sins. I believe in Your sacrifice. Thank You for paying for my sins and giving me eternal life in heaven.*

Journal Question: What are you relying on for eternal life?

_____

_____

_____

_____

DAY 2

What should I do when I'm harassed for my faith?

Today's Teen: Abel
Today's Action Verse: 2 Timothy 3:12
Storyline: Genesis 4

Abel Speaks Today: *"It's better to die for your faith than to live for nothing."*

Digging Deeper: Did you know Abel was the world's first martyr? Abel was a young man who lived out his faith and paid the ultimate price.

The Bible doesn't record or suggest this, but I wonder what impact tension between Abel and his brother Cain might have had on Abel before and after Abel performed his sacrifice. I wonder if Abel had any thoughts of compromising his offering so that his brother Cain wouldn't be angry.

The fact is that Abel chose commitment to God. And then his brother killed him.

This reminds me of the persecution some Christians face. Christians in the United States don't face persecution as severe as that faced by believers in other countries. But if you've been a believer for any length of time, you know how it feels to be mocked for your faith. Sometimes the heat comes from other Christians who think you're a little too passionate. That's OK, though. What really matters is what God thinks.

As was the case with Abel, your ultimate reward is heaven. If you suffer for your faith because you are honoring God, you can be sure this honors the Lord. Bible teacher M. R. DeHaan once said, "To come to Christ costs nothing, to follow Christ costs something, but to serve Christ costs everything."

Just Like You: When the New Year started, Sarah decided she was going to church every Sunday—no matter what. That meant she had to drop out of cheerleading practice. When she made this decision, everyone thought she was crazy. Even some of her Christian friends thought she was taking her spiritual walk a little too far. After all, she had the rest of her life to get serious.

But Sarah hung tough and did what she knew was right. She lost some of her friends on the cheerleading team—teammates she thought were close friends. Sarah felt hurt and alone. She was racked by doubt: *Did I make the right decision? It would be so much easier to go back.*

Then Sarah read Jesus's words to His disciples, *"If any man will come after me, let him deny himself, and take up his cross, and follow me"* (Matthew 16:24).

Did You Know? More Christians were put to death for their faith in the last century than in all other centuries combined.

Today's Prayer: *Lord, help me to do right, even if it costs me something. I know I may lose some things—friends, a position, maybe even a job. But I know that You will bless me in the long run if I do what I know is right.*

Journal Question: How do you react when someone ridicules your beliefs?

_____

_____

_____

_____

_____

_____

_____

_____

DAY 3

Can I afford to ignore "small" sins?

Today's Teen: Cain
Today's Action Verse: James 1:15
Storyline: Genesis 4

Cain Speaks Today: *"If you allow resentment to build in your soul, it may motivate you to do something you regret."*

Digging Deeper: I don't want to believe that Cain began with the intent to kill his brother. But a tiny seed of envy festered and grew within his heart. Soon his envy became a rage that was out of control. God even warned Cain that sin was lying at the doorstep of his heart and that he should take action to rule over it (Genesis 4:7). But pride kept Cain from making things right.

Big problems often start small: maybe a spirit of jealousy, seemingly innocent cheating in school, or even "harmless" surfing on questionable Web sites.

If Cain had dealt with sin when it was small, he would have avoided so much trouble. God was ready to forgive Cain. And just think, Abel would have lived. Instead, Abel died and Cain was messed up for life.

Be careful of sin, even "little" sins, in your life. When sin goes unchecked and unconfessed, it destroys you and the people you love.

Just Like You: Kacie Woody lived in the harmless, sleepy little town of Greenbrier, Arkansas. Like most teens, Kacie enjoyed spending time online.

Because of her outgoing personality, she liked to meet new friends. Chat rooms and social networking sites gave her a great opportunity for that.

One day while in a Christian chat room, she met a guy who went by the name of Dave. Over a few months, they struck up a cyber relationship. The closer they grew, the more Kacie began sharing personal details with Dave; she gave him her phone number and mapped out directions to her house.

As it turned out, Dave was not an innocent Christian teen but a 47-year-old man from California. One night in December 2002, Kacie's brother came home and found that Kacie was missing. It was soon discovered that she'd been kidnapped. The FBI came on the scene and, within a few days, tracked down this Dave guy. They followed his trail to a storage facility. Inside, they found a grisly scene. Dave had not only murdered Kacie, but he'd shot himself too.

Like many people, Kacie thought her Internet activity was safe, but she was too trusting of people she didn't know. (Information gathered from the October 2004 issue of *The Family Room,* FamilyLife's online magazine, www.FamilyLife.com/familyroom.)

The Internet can be a great source of information and communication, but it also can be a dangerous world, where predators lurk and sin awaits. If you want to guard your life and your purity, handle the Web with care and always maintain accountability.

Did You Know? Some important tips for online safety should be considered:

- Plead with your parents to set down strict guidelines, and ask them to keep you accountable.
- As tempting as chat rooms are, avoid them. Idle discussions can lead to unhealthy relationships.
- Ask your parents to buy and install a filter on your computer.
- Never give out personal contact information to people you do not know and have not met.
- Never download pictures from an unknown source.

Check out these Web sites for more Internet safety tips: fltoday.com, safekids.com, fbi.gov.

Today's Prayer: *Dear Lord, help me to deal with the subtle sins in my life. I know You are faithful to forgive me when I confess.*

Journal Question: Are you excusing some "little" sins in your life? If so, which ones? What can you do to eliminate these sins from your life?

_____

_____

_____

_____

_____

_____

✝ ✝ ✝ ✝ ✝ ✝ ✝ ✝ ✝   ✝ ✝ ✝ ✝ ✝ ✝ ✝ ✝ ✝

When I die, how will I be remembered?

Today's Teen: Abel
Today's Action Verse: Genesis 4:10
Storyline: Genesis 4

Abel Speaks Today: *"No matter how long you live, no matter how young you are, your life has a purpose."*

✝ ✝

Digging Deeper: A few years ago, two parents offered to sell naming rights for their newborn. Imagine: running around somewhere could be a little kid named Pepsi, Google, or iPod!

When the Bible was written, parents chose names that carried special meaning. When Eve gave birth to her firstborn, she chose the name Cain, saying, *"I have gotten a man from the LORD"* (Genesis 4:1). I wonder what she might have thought Cain's future as a man would be.

As for Abel, his name means "whisper" or "vanity." Eve was on target with this choice in one way, because Abel's life lasted a relatively short time, like a whisper. Yet, his days on earth resulted not in a whisper but in a loud statement, because Abel left a legacy of faithfulness and obedience (Genesis 4:4).

You can make a name for yourself, as Abel did, by living life with purpose. Ask yourself these questions: *If my life were cut short suddenly, have I left a legacy of obedience? How would I be remembered?*

It may seem like you're too young for such morbid talk, but Abel's life demonstrates that life is short. It's but a whisper. Only what you do for eternity will last.

Just Like You: In February 2006, Peter Wagler's parents received dreaded news from the Middle East. Their son, an 18-year-old army soldier, was killed when a homemade bomb exploded near his Abrams tank. Peter was a Christian and had been proud to serve his country.

Before he left, Peter had given his parents a sealed envelope with a letter to be opened if he died. In this letter, Peter said, "I would rather live my life fully and die young than live a long and boring life."

Like Abel, Peter found that a person's life is not measured in days or weeks or years, but in what he gives. What legacy are you leaving behind?

Did You Know? Some scholars believe that Abel lived approximately 120 years, which sounds like a lot, but it was actually a very short life when you consider that people at that time lived to be 700, 800, even 900 years old!

Today's Prayer: *Lord fill me with a sense of purpose. Help me live each day as if it were my last. Even though I am young, I want to impact my world.*

Journal Question: How can you make a difference in someone's life today?

_____

_____

_____

_____

_____

_____

_____

_____

_____

_____

✢ ✢ ✢ ✢ ✢ ✢ ✢ ✢ ✢  ✢ ✢ ✢ ✢ ✢ ✢ ✢ ✢ ✢

Why does God demand we love Him more than anyone else?

Today's Teen: Isaac
Today's Action Verse: Genesis 22:9
Storyline: Genesis 22

Isaac Speaks Today: *"Faith in God is serious stuff, and sometimes God will test your faith beyond what you think you can do."*

✢ ✢

Digging Deeper: I think Isaac must have known that he was born for a special purpose. He was the miracle child of Abraham and Sarah! Imagine the pressure and responsibility this suggests.

Nothing—and no one but God—could have prepared him, though, for the incredible moment when he and his father were at the place of sacrifice on Mount Moriah. Isaac originally had thought they were doing their usual sacrifices, but God had a big test lined up for Abraham and, I think, Isaac. Would Abraham be willing to give up his miracle son, whom he dearly loved? And would Isaac submit to lay down his life for God?

However, God never really intended for Abraham to offer Isaac. He was only trying Abraham to show how much he loved God. Did he love God more than his own son?

Hopefully you will never have to come this close to being a human sacrifice, but God will bring tests into your life. The trials you face—both big and little—can reveal to you just how much you trust Him.

It may be easy to say you love Jesus. It can be easy to talk about your great faith. But what about when it costs you something? That's where the rubber meets the road.

Just Like You: Is it hard for you to understand how God could ask Abraham to give up Isaac as a sacrifice? Do you think God was cruel to expect this, especially since Isaac was a miracle child?

God really didn't intend for Abraham to kill Isaac—He just wanted Abraham to give up control. God asks the same thing of us. It's called radical faith. Jesus Himself said, *"If any man come to me, and hate not his father, and mother, and wife, and children, and brethren, and sisters, yea, and his own life also, he **cannot** be my **disciple**"* (Luke 14:26; bold added).

Does this mean you should actually hate your mom, dad, brother, and sister? No! God wants to confirm that He has first place in your life. And when He does, it's amazing how your love for your mom, dad, brothers, sisters, and friends will grow.

What does all this mean? Here are some ways that you might be tempted to put your loved ones in the place of God:

- You buy your best friend a really cool birthday gift with the money you had planned to put in the offering on Sunday.
- You take your brother or sister to a ball game and blow off your youth-group meeting.
- You let your unbelieving relatives and family influence what you watch on TV, what music you listen to, and what you do with your free time.
- You give up your quiet time with God to hang out with friends.

Did You Know? Mount Moriah, where Abraham offered Isaac, is the same mountain where Jesus was offered for sin. When Abraham told Isaac, *"God will provide himself a lamb"* (Genesis 22:8), those words not only prophesied a lamb in the place of Isaac, they prophesied Jesus, who would be provided by God as the Perfect Lamb, who would come and take away the sins of the world.

Today's Prayer: *God, I don't ever want to allow my love for anyone or anything to get in the way of my love for You.*

Journal Question: Are you allowing a relationship or friendship to get in the way of your walk with God? If so, what changes can you make?

_____

_____

_____

_____

_____

_____

_____

_____

_____

_____

_____

_____

_____

_____

_____

_____

Why should I marry a Christian?

Today's Teen: Isaac
Today's Action Verse: Genesis 24:7
Storyline: Genesis 24

Isaac Speaks Today: *"Waiting to marry someone who shares your values is really worth the wait."*

Digging Deeper: Isaac apparently understood the saying, "True love waits," because he didn't find the girl of his dreams *for 40 years.* Why? The reason, I pose, is because he wouldn't settle for a wife who was an unbeliever. At times, he may have felt tempted to start a relationship with an unbeliever, but the Bible gives no evidence that Isaac did. What is evident is that God blessed Isaac's faithfulness by miraculously bringing the beautiful Rebekah into his life. As soon as Isaac saw her, he knew she was worth the wait.

Isaac understood he couldn't be what is called *"unequally yoked"* with someone who didn't share his faith (2 Corinthians 6:14). That probably sounds a lot like advice your parents and pastor have given you. It may sound old-fashioned and probably doesn't seem to make sense. You may even think that you could get away with dating someone who is not a Christian and try to convert him or her, which is sometimes called "missionary dating." This might happen, but more likely, this type of relationship will end in devastating failure.

Maybe your situation is like Isaac's. Maybe there aren't many young people of your faith in your school, church, or community. It's so tempting to just lower your standards and date someone who seems to be nice, but doesn't share your faith. However, it is important to wait for a Christian who loves the Lord, especially if you want God to bless you with someone as right for you as Rebekah and Isaac were for each other.

Just Like You: Gavin is the only child in his family and the only young person in the tiny, small-town church where his family worships. At school, he has a few friends, but most of them are not believers—so most of the people he hangs around with are older.

Gavin has never had a problem hanging out with older people—but he often wonders about finding someone to date and possibly marry (way down the road of life).

Ashley lives a few blocks away and is a pretty good kid. She's stayed out of trouble and gets good grades. Ashley has even made it known a few times how much she enjoys spending time with Gavin.

But Gavin knows he can't get serious with Ashley because she's not a Christian. He's tried hard to get her to come to church, but she continues to brush him off. Even Gavin's parents have prayed for Ashley to become a believer, but she just really doesn't want to have anything to do with Christianity.

Sometimes Gavin lies awake at night wondering why God doesn't bring more Christian girls into his town and his church. But then he remembers the story of Isaac and thinks, *OK, God, I'm still pretty young, and if I'm faithful, I know you'll show me the way.*

Did You Know? Why did Abraham send his servant to find Isaac a wife? In those days, the father, or patriarch of the family, would find or appoint a person to find a suitable wife for his son and negotiate the terms with the girl's family.

Today's Prayer: *Dear Lord, I know the dangers of "missionary dating." Help me to trust you and seek guidance before getting involved in a serious relationship.*

Journal Question: Are you putting God first in serious relationships? How do you know you are doing this?

_____

_____

_____

_____

_____

_____

_____

_____

Who am I when no one is looking?

Today's Teen: Rebekah
Today's Action Verses: Genesis 24:13–16
Storyline: Genesis 24

Rebekah Speaks Today: _"God often speaks to you on ordinary days and in ordinary ways."_

Digging Deeper: Rebekah didn't realize the importance of this particular trip to the well. It was an ordinary task on an ordinary day. The servant was just another traveler in need of a cool drink. What was it about Rebekah that so impressed the tired, old man? She was beautiful, pure, innocent,...and willing to go beyond simple courtesy to help a complete stranger.

Anyone can primp or get to looking mighty fine for a first date. Anyone can put on his or her best behavior for a teacher or coach. Anyone can freshen up for an important interview. But what about those chance encounters when you're caught off guard? If people saw you on an ordinary day, would they be impressed? Would they see something different about you?

Rebekah didn't simply put on the spirituality "for the cameras." She wasn't playing to the crowd. She didn't schmooze the important people. No, she had an inner beauty that radiated to those around her no matter what time of day it was.

Just Like You: *What's with that girl?* Lynda wondered each time she saw Debbie. *She can't be in her right mind. A teenager can't be that happy when she isn't even popular! Duh, she doesn't even have a boyfriend! I'm not popular, but I know better than to be happy about it!* Lynda wanted to say, "You have no teen requirements for happiness, so quit being happy, already!"

Lynda had to figure Debbie out, so she initiated conversation. Over the weeks, she learned things weren't always good for Debbie, but she didn't become discouraged or angry.

One day Lynda blurted, "Why are you always happy?"

Debbie answered, "The problems don't get me down because I know I'm going to heaven one day."

Wasn't Debbie a little presumptuous to say she knew she was going to heaven? Debbie didn't think she was better than anyone else. How could she be so sure?

"How do you know you're going to heaven?" Lynda asked.

Debbie explained, "Jesus died for my sins so I wouldn't have to pay for them. I'm going to heaven because I've accepted what He did for me."

Lynda still didn't really get it, but Debbie helped her to understand by sharing some books and taking her to church. Lynda eventually came to Christ. Debbie was just different enough to make Lynda wonder why she was different. (Story provided by Sandra Holmes McGarrity, who lives and writes in Chesapeake, Virginia. Visit her Web page at http://hometown.aol.com/mygr8m8/myhomepage/books.html.)

Did You Know? In biblical times, it was customary for women, especially young girls, to collect water for the entire family—once in the morning and once at night. A rope with a bucket was used to reach deep into the well.

The water was then poured into large clay pitchers that were carried home on the head or shoulders.

Today's Prayer: *Dear God, help me to live for You on those ordinary days when it seems as though nothing big is happening.*

Journal Question: In what way can you reflect Christ today to those who don't know you or Him?

_____

_____

_____

_____

_____

_____

_____

_____

_____

_____

_____

_____

_____

_____

_____

_____

_____

DAY 8

How do I attract a good Christian guy or girl?

Today's Teen: Rebekah
Today's Action Verse: Genesis 24:12
Storyline: Genesis 24

Rebekah Speaks Today: *"You may find the right person to marry when you're least expecting it."*

Digging Deeper: Popular magazines, novels, and TV dramas all seem to want you to think that they have the right answers when it comes to attracting a good guy or girl. But you might be surprised to know that Rebekah had all the answers, even 4,000 years ago. She attracted a soul mate without trying at all—as should be the case.

It's not that Rebekah didn't care how she looked. In fact, the Bible talks about her rare beauty. But her life wasn't consumed with her looks or with trying to attract a guy. Her life was consumed with serving others and God. Her physical appearance was not flawed by her character. She evidently spent more time working on her inner beauty than her outer beauty.

And guess what? Rebekah was exactly the type of girl Isaac wanted and his father's servant went looking for. He wasn't looking for someone obsessively boy crazy or a flirt. He was looking for something different.

It's hard not to be consumed in finding or maintaining relationships. It's hard not to spend your entire high school years in anxious worry about who likes you or whom you like. But God has a much better way: the worry-free path of obedience, trust, and gentle grace.

Just Like You: OK, so you say that you're not worried about finding the perfect person, but you're not planning on becoming a monk or a nun either. So you wonder, *How exactly do I go about attracting a godly young man or woman?* Here are a few things that worked for Rebekah:

- **Don't try to be noticed.** Rebekah wasn't asking for attention. She was just doing her job. She didn't hide, but she didn't go out of her way to try to get noticed either.
- **Make every day count.** Rebekah must have made it a point to look nice each and every trip to the well. She always brought her best personality, attitude, and appearance.
- **Guard your purity.** Abraham's servant immediately sensed Rebekah's purity. Purity encompassed who she was as a woman. This purity made her more attractive for the man God would bring across her path.
- **Put others first.** Often those who give the most to serve others seem to experience blessings as a result. Don't be so obsessed with pursuing a godly mate that you edge and elbow yourself to the front of every line, on every stage, and into every supposedly cool crowd. Instead, let your service do the talking.

Did You Know? In the tough terrain of the Arabian Desert, camels are valuable assets. They can carry a lot of weight and can go for days without water, storing it up in their humps and rationing it as they need the water.

Today's Prayer: *Dear God, help me to become the godly man or woman You would have me to be. I trust You to lead me to godly people to befriend and then, one day, to the person I will marry.*

Journal Question: Am I the kind of person that a godly Christian would be interested in? What areas of my life need improvement to make me closer to God first, and then more spiritually attractive to others?

_____

_____

_____

_____

_____

_____

_____

_____

_____

_____

_____

✛ ✛ ✛ ✛ ✛ ✛ ✛ ✛ ✛   ✛ ✛ ✛ ✛ ✛ ✛ ✛ ✛ ✛

Does it matter how I treat someone who can't possibly help me?

Today's Teen: Rebekah
Today's Action Verse: Genesis 24:18
Storyline: Genesis 24

Rebekah Speaks Today: *"An attitude of service on an ordinary day may change your life forever."*

✛ ✛

Digging Deeper: True service, it is said, is helping people without expecting anything in return. This was Rebekah's practice. She went all out to help a weary stranger on an ordinary day. Not only did she willingly give him her water, but also she went back to draw water for his camels. This was a hard job that must have left her feeling exhausted.

Rebekah didn't know her kindness toward the stranger, Abraham's servant, would bring her to her future husband. She had no motives behind her service, and yet she was rewarded.

Service without strings attached is the service God blesses. It's so tempting to charm the people who can affect our lives, such as the principal, the pastor, or your parents. You may even do special things for that cute team captain or lead cheerleader. But what about someone who can't really do anything for you? What about the kid who gets bad grades? What about the guy with acne or the girl with the big glasses? Hey, what about the old lady who struggles to take her garbage out or clean her yard? Jesus let us know that whatever we do unto the least of these, we do it unto Him (Matthew 25:40).

Just Like You: How can a young person be a servant? You might be saying to yourself, *I don't want to be anyone's slave.* But servanthood is not slavery. Putting others first doesn't require you to give up who you are and the courage to be the person God has intended for you to be. Here is what true service looks like:

- **Going the extra mile:** Are you willing to go the extra mile for someone in need, such as the elderly neighbor who needs his or her grass cut in the summer or the driveway shoveled in the wintertime?
- **Putting others first:** When you get home from a long, hard day at school, do you give your parents a list of demands, or are you willing to put them first—find out what you can do to help them—even if you're tired?
- **Taking time to help:** If a classmate needs help with a tough assignment, are you willing take the time needed to help that person?
- **Sacrificing your plans to meet others' needs:** When someone has a real emergency—broken-down car, power outage, sick or injured family member—are you willing to sacrifice your plans for the day to meet his or her needs?

Did You Know? Bible teacher Warren Wiersbe, in his book *Be Obedient,* says, "Watering ten camels is no easy job! After a long trek, a thirsty camel might drink as much as forty gallons of water; and Rebekah had to draw all that water by hand."

Today's Prayer: *God, please help me to take advantage of opportunities to serve "the least of these."*

Journal Question: Whom can I encourage today simply by serving them—with no strings attached? How can I serve them?

_____

_____

_____

_____

_____

_____

✛ ✛ ✛ ✛ ✛ ✛ ✛ ✛ ✛ ✛   ✛ ✛ ✛ ✛ ✛ ✛ ✛ ✛ ✛

Who am I on an ordinary day?

Today's Teen: Rebekah
Today's Action Verses: Genesis 24:26–28
Storyline: Genesis 24

Rebekah Speaks Today: *"When you put others first, you might be their answer to prayer."*

✛ ✛

Digging Deeper: Have you ever been an answer to someone's prayer? Rebekah was, and she didn't even know it. Don't think that what happened to her that day was some kind of accident! No, Rebekah's life was marked by a combination of God's will and her choices.

Was Rebekah simply lucky? No way! Rebekah came to this place in her life because she had carefully cultivated character that would be attractive to a godly man like Isaac. She had not wasted her teen years in idle daydreaming, excessive partying, or wasteful habits. And because of her choices and God's faithfulness, she enjoyed the blessing of experiencing God's best for her future.

Let's take a quick look at two myths about Christianity. One is that you're supposed to sit around, and God will work everything out. The other is that God has nothing to do with your life, and you're supposed to follow a list of rules for success. Neither is right.

Rebekah's story shows that God works through our good choices. Your life is a partnership with God: Your choices do have rewards and consequences; but God also intervenes with His grace and works miracles to help you accomplish His will.

Just Like You: By keeping your focus, you, too, could be the answer to someone's prayer. Rebekah made three key choices that helped place her in the center of God's will:

- **Rebekah chose to be a hard worker.** The twice-daily trips to the well were not easy. The trip was probably several miles, and drawing the water required arduous work. Rebekah didn't shy away from hard work.
- **Rebekah chose to be a virgin.** She guarded her moral purity as a treasure. She was saving herself for the man God would bring into her life.
- **Rebekah chose to be a servant.** She didn't *have to* offer water to the servant. She didn't *have to* bring water to each of his camels. But she did because her heart was focused on the needs of others.

Did You Know? Wells were a common gathering place for travelers. Like a truck stop on an American highway, the well was where ancient travelers would stop, water their camels, get directions, seek lodging, and find out more about the new town.

Today's Prayer: *God, please help me to serve others, even on ordinary days when I don't feel like it.*

Journal Question: How can I be the answer to someone's prayers today?

_____

_____

_____

_____

_____

_____

_____

_____

_____

_____

_____

✢ ✢ ✢ ✢ ✢ ✢ ✢ ✢ ✢  ✢ ✢ ✢ ✢ ✢ ✢ ✢ ✢

Does it matter *when* I begin to live for God?

Today's Teen: Rebekah
Today's Action Verse: Genesis 24:58
Storyline: Genesis 24

Rebekah Speaks Today: *"When God opens a door, don't delay. Walk right through it."*

✢ ✢

Digging Deeper: In a matter of a few hours, Rebekah's entire future was handed to her on a silver platter. Can you imagine what might have gone through her mind? Would she be sent with Abraham's servant? Who would take care of her? Should she wait ten days or go right away? Unlike most women in that culture, Rebekah was presented with a choice: She could leave immediately or wait a period of days. Sensing God's divine will, she decided to leave immediately—home, family, and everything she knew—to go and marry a man she had never met.

Hesitation often leads to second-guessing. When God provides an opportunity, it is best to grab hold of it and go forward. When God opens a door, it's best to walk through it.

Too often, young people pledge to serve God, but to do it later—maybe after they've gotten all the partying and fun out of their systems, or maybe after they've sown their wild oats. But later may never come.

If God is calling you, follow Him now.

Just Like You: A *Focus on the Family* broadcast shared the story of Joshua Youssef, the son of famous radio preacher and theologian Michael Youssef. Joshua became a Christian at the age of seven and knew that God was calling him into the ministry.

When Joshua was in college, he began to run away from God. During his senior year, he began to engage in all kinds of activities that he knew were wrong, but he continued down this path because he wanted to escape the Lord's call upon his life.

One day, the Lord got Joshua's attention in a dramatic way. Joshua and three other daredevil friends went white-water rafting on a dangerous section of the Tallapoosa River called the Falls, near a hydroelectric dam. One of his friends nearly drowned and another was trapped in a *hydraulic* (a term for the whirlpool effect created when water moves over a rock at a high rate of speed).

Joshua was able to get out of the river and run back to his car for help. On his way back from the hospital, he realized that God was trying to get his attention. At that moment, he made a covenant with God to serve Him, in whatever capacity, for the rest of his life.

Did You Know? Rebekah's brother, Laban, seemed to be the main negotiator in her marriage to Isaac. Despite the fact that her father's name was mentioned in the decision making (Genesis 24:50), many scholars think her father may have been dead already. Regardless of whether the father was alive or dead, Laban was obviously the leader of the family at that time and had the authority to decide whom Rebekah would marry.

Today's Prayer: *Dear God, help me to live for You **now.** Please show me where and how I can serve You today.*

Journal Question: What doors might God be opening for you? What opportunities are available right now?

_____

_____

_____

_____

_____

_____

_____

_____

_____

_____

_____

_____

_____

_____

_____

_____

_____

_____

_____

_____

_____

_____

_____

_____

DAY 12

If I step out on faith, will God take care of me?

Today's Teen: Rebekah
Today's Action Verse: Genesis 24:61
Storyline: Genesis 24

Rebekah Speaks Today: *"When you take a leap of faith, you can be sure God will be with you."*

Digging Deeper: As the camel caravan carried Rebekah away from her home, past well wishers who wanted to see her greatly blessed, imagine the nervous feeling she might have had in the pit of her stomach. Would she have thought, *Am I crazy or what?* Here she was, leaving her family and everything she knew to go marry a man she had never met. Now that's some kind of faith!

You'll probably never have to marry a person you don't know—and that's a good thing! But it still takes faith to follow God's will in your relationships. It's easy to give in to pressure. It's a challenge to not give up your purity; it takes faith to stand tall and save your purity for marriage. It's easy to get involved in a relationship with an unbeliever; it takes faith to wait for a godly person to come along. It's easy to dress like everyone else; it takes faith to spend a little extra money and time to find modest clothes. It's easy to watch movies and read magazines that present sexual temptations; it takes faith to guard your heart against impurity of the mind.

Just Like You: Spending three months away from her family, her friends, and all the comforts of home seemed a little scary for Beth, but she felt God wanted her to volunteer for a summer missions project in Louisiana. It all started when she was reading one of her favorite Christian magazines. An advertisement stated a missions agency was seeking young people who were willing to give up their summer to help rebuild the homes of poor people affected by Katrina. At first she thought, *But I don't know anything about building and construction.* But then the next sentence said, "No trade experience required." *Hmm, maybe I could do this,* was her next thought.

After talking with her parents and pastor, Beth decided to do it. This would be her way of helping less fortunate people. And she relished the opportunity to grow in her faith. The organization would pay her expenses, so she didn't have to raise money. That meant she could start right away. Beth wasn't sure what to expect, but she knew God would be with her and protect her.

Did You Know? The journey from Rebekah's hometown to Isaac's hometown was 500 miles and probably took two months to travel.

Today's Prayer: *God, give me courage to deal with not only the known and expected things in life but also the unknown and unexpected things.*

Journal Question: How is God testing your faith? How will you react to sudden and unplanned circumstances He orchestrates?

_____

_____

_____

_____

_____

_____

_____

_____

_____

_____

_____

DAY 13

What should I give up to make my friends like me?

Today's Teen: Esau
Today's Action Verses: Hebrews 12:16–17
Storyline: Genesis 25:20–34

Esau Speaks Today: *"Making impulsive choices based on your feelings at the moment may lead to a lifetime of regret."*

Digging Deeper: Have you ever been extremely hungry? For Esau, a bowl of stew had never looked so good. The more his brother negotiated, the hungrier Esau grew. He didn't care what he had to give up. When those steaming hot lentils reached his tongue, he probably thought the soup was worth that birthright.

But was the satisfaction of immediate food *really* worth the birthright? Esau had traded something precious for a few moments of pleasure—temporary satisfaction that would be gone in less than an hour.

In his book, *The Purity Principle,* Randy Alcorn says this: "Those who turn from God to embrace a God-substitute suffer terrible loss. Why? Because they were made to find joy in God, not the substitute. They swap God's present and future blessing for something they can immediately see, taste, or feel. But that something never satisfies."

You have to ask yourself several questions: *Am I willing to take that risk? Am I willing to gamble on my own future for temporary satisfaction? Am I willing to live with the consequences of a rash decision?*

Even though God's grace can cover many sins, it's better to heed warning signs and advice from parents, pastors, and friends. Josh Billings says, "One-half the troubles of this life can be traced to saying yes too quickly and not saying no soon enough."

Just Like You: What do you do when temptation seems hard to resist? Here are three important steps you can take to overcome the temptation to partake of the devil's "bowls of soup":

1. **Guard your eyes (Proverbs 4:25).** As soon as Esau's gaze centered on that stew, it was over. Temptation begins in the eyes, travels to the heart, and soon activates the hard-to-control impulses of the body. Don't even glance at questionable magazines or Web sites. Avoid TV shows, movies, or songs that encourage you to give in to temptation.

2. **Feed your soul (Psalm 119:9).** Caught up in the thrill of hunting season, Esau must have missed one too many meals. By the time he stumbled back home, he was weak and hungry. Likewise, when you neglect the feeding of your spirit, as Esau did, you're vulnerable to temptation. Make sure you get a daily dose of God's Word to keep your spiritual defenses strong. When you begin to feel weak, stop and pray.

3. **Set boundaries.** Esau's birthright was his for the keeping; that fact was nonnegotiable. But he gave it away without consideration, without hesitation. What about you? When you decide in advance on what activities are out of bounds, you'll be stronger when the opportunity for compromise is presented. Have you drawn a line in the sand when it comes to certain activities? Have you established boundaries?

Did You Know? In the days of Jacob and Esau, the father, by tradition, passed the birthright and blessing to the oldest son. The blessing could be bartered away, or it could be taken away if the elder son shamed his father.

Today's Prayer: *God, give me the strength to do what is right when tempted. Help me to be guided not by temporary feelings but by Your Holy Spirit.*

Journal Question: What "God substitutes" are tempting you today?

_____

_____

_____

_____

_____

_____

In what ways may I be exploiting my friends?

Today's Teen: Jacob
Today's Action Verse: 1 Timothy 2:9
Storyline: Genesis 25:29–34

Jacob Speaks Today: *"Taking advantage of your friends ends up hurting those you love and you as well."*

Digging Deeper: Esau was vulnerable, and Jacob knew it. Jacob desperately wanted Esau's birthright and employed a series of schemes to get it.

Was it a coincidence that Jacob just happened to be creating a big batch of delicious stew when Esau strolled in from the field? Maybe; maybe not. I think Jacob might have carefully hatched this plot. Jacob probably knew his brother's weakness and exploited it for his own gain.

Do young people today take advantage of friends for personal gain or enjoyment? Yes. Young people often do this with their bodies. Girls and guys can easily lure each other by wearing suggestive clothes, making it hard for the other gender to battle lust. They can take advantage of each other by using flattery and all kinds of attention. But true friends carefully guard their friends' purity rather than exploiting their weaknesses.

Just Like You: Ella Gunderson of Redmond, Washington, was fed up with the clothing selection at her nearby department store. So she wrote a letter to the local Nordstrom store, asking them to offer a more modest clothing line for young girls like herself.

Her letter, which made it all the way to the top executives at Nordstrom, had this to say: "Dear Nordstrom, I am an eleven-year-old girl who has tried shopping at your store for clothes (in particular jeans), but all of them ride way under my hips, and the next size up is too big and falls down.

"I see all of these girls who walk around with pants that show their belly button and underwear," she continued. "Your clerks suggest that there is only one look. If that is true, then girls are supposed to walk around half naked. I think that you should change that."

The department store chain was so shocked, they wrote Ella back, promising to offer a wider array of clothing styles. Other stores soon got wind of it and contacted Ella as well and also promised to offer more modest apparel. Ella eventually appeared on *The Today Show* and other news outlets, speaking up for young girls who don't want to dress seductively.

From a very early age, Ella chose modesty, and it wasn't because of lack of a sense of style. There is *power* in physical and emotional purity.

Did You Know? *Parenting Today's Adolescent,* by radio broadcaster Dennis Rainey and his wife, Barbara, states the following about young ladies and the way they dress: "Especially when young, they don't understand consciously how accentuating certain parts of the body affects boys and men. Boys do pay more attention to a more enticing appearance. That's enjoyable for girls, so they may lean even more toward this kind of dress to attract even more attention. They don't fully realize the values they are portraying and what type of boys they're wooing."

Today's Prayer: *Dear God, help me with my clothing choices. Help me send a strong message of purity to those around me, so I don't unintentionally trap others into making poor choices.*

Journal Question: How can you be an ally instead of an enemy in your friends' battles against lust and temptation?

_____

_____

_____

_____

_____

DAY 15

✛ ⊹ ✛ ✛ ✛ ✛ ✛ ✛ ✛   ✛ ⊹ ✛ ✛ ✛ ✛ ✛ ✛ ✛

Why should I get advice about a relationship with the opposite sex?

Today's Teen: Esau
Today's Action Verse: 1 John 2:16
Storyline: Genesis 26:34–35

Esau Speaks Today: *"A romantic relationship with an unbeliever is a really bad idea."*

✛ ⊹ ✛ ✛ ✛ ✛ ✛ ✛ ⊹ ✛ ✛ ✛ ✛ ✛ ✛ ✛ ⊹ ✛ ✛ ✛ ✛ ✛ ⊹

Digging Deeper: When it comes to relationships, God sets up clear boundaries. Abraham seemed to be aware of those boundaries, but Esau didn't. Abraham, Esau's grandfather, had set a standard for Esau's father,

Isaac, by searching for a wife for Isaac from his own tribe. But Esau did not uphold this standard. Esau wanted to do things his own way. He threw away boundaries and married two women from a heathen culture.

One purpose for God's boundaries is to help His people maintain a pure heart toward Him and avoid the influence of heathen cultures and idol worship. Today, God's boundaries for young people are not much different. Romantic relationships with unbelievers are unhealthy and could move your heart away from God. You could be tempted to follow Esau's path. So even if a relationship seems right, but the guy or girl is not a Christian or is not intent on following Christ, it's best to stay out of it.

When it comes to relationships, the advice of your parents and your pastor is very important. Believe it or not, they have been where you are right now, and they have wisdom from God. Seek their input. Trust them. Follow God's words.

Just Like You: Miriam couldn't keep her eyes off of Jack, the new guy at school. He was tall, athletic, and had a great personality. She sat by him during class, and they soon became friends.

Miriam's new interest worried her parents. First of all, they felt she was too young for a serious relationship. Secondly, they didn't think Jack was a good influence because he wasn't a believer.

At first, Miriam resented her parent's advice. It seemed they wanted to take away her fun. *Don't they want me to be happy?* she wondered.

Then Miriam learned one day about a longtime friend with whom she'd lost contact. Apparently, the friend had run off with her boyfriend against her parent's advice and had gotten pregnant. The baby's father left, leaving Miriam's friend to raise a young child by herself. It scared Miriam and made her think, *Maybe Mom and Dad have a point.*

Did You Know? When Esau chose his two wives, he broke an important family tradition. In that culture, the parents chose a mate for their son or daughter—often before he or she even met the future mate! While that seems extreme, it is a good idea for young people to receive input from godly parents.

Today's Prayer: *Dear Lord, give me wisdom in my relationships. Help me to follow the advice of wise parents, leaders, and mentors.*

Journal Question: Who are some leaders you can talk with about guy/girl issues?

_____

_____

_____

_____

✛ ✛ ✛ ✛ ✛ ✛ ✛ ✛   ✛ ✛ ✛ ✛ ✛ ✛ ✛ ✛

Should I ever stand up to authority?

Today's Teen: Jacob
Today's Action Verse: Genesis 27:8
Storyline: Genesis 27:6–46

Jacob Speaks Today: _"Your parents are usually right, but if what they ask of you means you are going to sin, you have a tough choice to make."_

✛ ✛ ✛ ✛ ✛ ✛ ✛ ✛ ✛ ✛ ✛ ✛ ✛ ✛ ✛ ✛ ✛ ✛ ✛

Digging Deeper: Conspire with Mom or remain honest before God and man? That's the situation Jacob faced. He loved his mother, and she preferred him over his brother. But she purposely encouraged Jacob to deceive his father. And Jacob went along with her program rather than stick with truth.

God hates disobedience. God also hates deceit. What happens when two biblical principles collide—obedience to authority versus honesty? Don't think this is always an easy choice. Surely Jacob thought about his deceitful actions and that he was doing wrong in God's sight.

What should you do when someone you trust tells you to do something you know is wrong? Well, the Bible says that you should always obey God first. This is not a blanket license for rebellion, because all authority should be treated with respect. But if someone in authority tells you to do wrong, it simply means that your allegiance to God always comes first. Put God first.

Just Like You: All spring, Rachel tried to get a summer job. She wanted to earn enough money for a fall missions trip to Brazil. She filled out a lot of applications, only to be rejected time and again. Nobody seemed to be hiring.

Finally, Rachel landed a job at the grocery store. It wasn't glamorous, but it would give her enough hours to earn the money she needed for the fall.

On her first day, Rachel walked into the break room to check the schedule. To her dismay, she saw that her boss had penciled her in for three Sundays in a row. She had already told him she couldn't work Sundays because of church, so she politely went to him and asked for a schedule change. He gave her a rather curt answer. She was new and if she wanted to keep her job, she would have to work Sundays.

Now what? she thought. *I can't do this, but I also need to earn money. Lord, what do I do?* Then Rachel remembered a verse she'd read in Proverbs that morning before rushing out the door: *"Trust in the LORD with all thine heart; and lean not unto thine own understanding"* (Proverbs 3:5). *OK, Lord. I can do this. You'll take care of me.*

Rachel walked out of the break room, apron in hand. She politely told her boss that she couldn't work for him because church was that important.

Did You Know? The spiritual blessing passed down from Isaac to Jacob was a God-given heritage. Once Isaac gave it to Jacob, it couldn't be rescinded.

Today's Prayer: *Dear God, please give me the courage to stand for You—even if it means disobeying authorities. Help me to do what's right, even when it costs me something.*

Journal Question: In what areas of your life might you have to stand up to someone in authority? And if such a case arises, how can you approach the situation with grace?

_____

_____

_____

_____

_____

_____

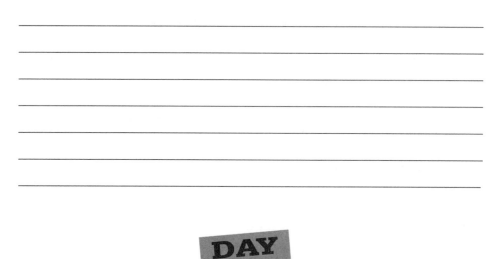

DAY 17

Do the choices I'm making now really matter?

Today's Teen: Esau
Today's Action Verse: Genesis 27:38
Storyline: Genesis 27:30–41

Esau Speaks Today: *"Remember your choices do have consequences."*

Digging Deeper: As Esau stood by his father, Isaac, the bad choices he had made flashed through his mind. He stood there, a broken and bitter man.

Was he sorry he traded away his birthright? Was he upset over disappointing his parents and his Lord? Maybe he was. But whether or not he was sorry, he was most likely, or should I say, *for sure*, sad and mad—mad at Jacob for having taken both his birthright and his blessing.

Esau wanted all of the perks that come with a spiritual life, but without making any investments. He wanted all the gain without any of the pain. But the law of sowing and reaping caught up with him.

That law hasn't changed since Esau's time. If you fill your life with good influences like the Bible, prayer, godly advice, and good friends, then your life will be marked by wisdom. However, if you are influenced only by popular music, movies, TV shows, and worldly friends, then your life will be marked by foolishness.

Now is a good time to start planting good seeds—seeds that will one day reap an enjoyable harvest.

Just Like You: When Shane started his freshman year of high school, he, unlike his friends, determined to study hard and stay out of trouble. Shane took some tougher courses and really paid attention in class.

Shane's friends didn't understand why he wouldn't hang out with them more or why he wouldn't sneak out of the house in the middle of the night to go places with them. By the time his junior year rolled around, Shane was ready to look at colleges. One day, his mom took him and a buddy to a university near his house. After interviewing some of the professors, Shane, his friend, and his mom stopped in the admissions office. The admissions office personnel looked at Shane's records and were thrilled to have him as a prospective student. However, when they looked at his friend's records, they encouraged him to take a crash course in math and science his senior year and to wait two years; then maybe he would be accepted.

Shane was grateful he had worked hard and taken his responsibilities seriously during his freshman year; now he was beginning to experience the fruit of his labors. On the other hand, his buddy now wished he had taken school more seriously, as Shane had.

Did You Know? Very few trees are as beautiful as the oak. Its wood is highly sought after for flooring, furniture, and carvings. The oak starts as a tiny acorn, growing until a deep root system develops that will allow it to stand strong through the storms. If you plant an oak tree, you will have to live a long time to see it fully mature.

Today's Prayer: *Lord, help me to plant good seeds early in life so I will have good fruit to enjoy in the coming years.*

Journal Question: What are some choices you're making now that may have an impact on the rest of your life? What are some of the possible consequences?

_____

_____

_____

_____

_____

_____

Does God really care if I'm lonely or afraid?

Today's Teen: Jacob
Today's Action Verse: Jeremiah 33:3
Storyline: Genesis 28:11–22

Jacob Speaks Today: *"When you feel all alone, you can be sure God is right there with you."*

Digging Deeper: For the first time, Jacob was alone. He was out from under the secure umbrella of all that was familiar. He was beginning a frightening new chapter in his life.

Jacob's first night away, God revealed Himself to Jacob, promising to him, as He did to Abraham, the land he was on and abundant descendents through whom all people would be blessed. The Lord then told Jacob He was with him and would keep him everywhere he went. It was a powerful reminder that Jacob might be miles away from his family, but he was never far away from God.

God's promise to Jacob is also available to you. He's never more than a prayer away.

Soon you may be away from familiar surroundings, plunging into new challenges, such as college, the missions field, or new avenues of ministry. Your heavenly Father is and will be with you. He'll be with you in the dorm room, in the break room, on the practice field, and in the classroom. He'll be there to guide and comfort you through your highs and lows.

As you start making your way, run *to* God, not *away from* Him. Now, more than ever, you need the reassurance of the Holy Spirit, infusing your heart with strength, filling your mind with wisdom, and empowering your soul to fulfill God's will.

D. L. Moody said, "He who kneels the most stands best." So do what it takes to stand.

Just Like You: Has your quiet time been either nonexistent or somewhat boring? Maybe you're not getting anything from your reading. Here are a few tips:

- **Don't start with Leviticus.** That sounds like a no-brainer, but some people start in the really difficult books and then toss their Bibles a few days and a thousand "cubits" and funny names later. Try reading through the book of John or any of the Gospels. Then work your way through the New Testament and the Book of Psalms.

- **Try a helpful study Bible,** like *The Daily Walk Bible, Extreme Teen Bible,* or *Student's Life Application Bible.* These offer helpful side notes and give you background information on some of the people in the Bible.

- **Focus on meditation, not on volume.** Some days you may read only one verse—but that verse sticks with you and makes you think. Other days you may read several chapters. Remember, it's not competition; it's not a reading contest. The idea is to hear what God is saying to your heart.

- **Pray over the key passage you've read.** Write down some questions you can ask yourself about it. Keep a journal of your thoughts.

- **Be still and listen to God's still, gentle voice.** Find a place away from the hustle and bustle of life where you can experience what God is saying to you, and *be sure* to write that down.

Did You Know? Jacob called the special place where he met God *Bethel*. This word means "house of God." For Jacob, this was holy ground, a sacred place that would always serve as a special memorial for an important chapter in his life.

Today's Prayer: *Lord, guide me through each new chapter of my life. I know that You are always with me wherever I go.*

Journal Question: In what moments or circumstances do you feel the most abandoned by God? What truths could you recall to encourage your heart in such moments?

_____

_____

_____

_____

_____

_____

_____

_____

_____

_____

_____

_____

_____

Does God care about me— even if I'm not popular?

Today's Teen: Leah

Today's Action Verses: Psalm 139:13–16

Storyline: Genesis 29

Leah Speaks Today: *"Even if you've struggled to live up to someone else's expectations, you can always rest in God's love."*

Digging Deeper: Two girls fighting over one guy. Sound familiar? Way back in the Old Testament, two sisters, Leah and Rachel, fought bitterly over one guy—Jacob. The girls' father had convinced Leah, the older and less-popular sister, to take part in a bizarre and dishonest scheme to become Jacob's wife. But Jacob had already given his whole heart and soul to Rachel, the younger one. So Leah was on the losing end of the fight. She knew what it meant to be rejected for someone else. Compared with Rachel, Leah was sort of ordinary. All this left Leah feeling unwanted.

Maybe you feel a little like Leah: rejected, second fiddle, out of place in this world. Maybe you're not a stud athlete, a cover-girl type, an honors student, or one of the most popular girls or guys in school. But here's some good news: God doesn't see you as ordinary. In fact, He created you—special and unique—for a specific purpose. There are no accidents with God—only miracles.

Just Like You: You are probably tired of comparing yourself with other people and wishing you were a little taller, a little skinnier, a little wealthier, or just born in a different family. But the truth is that God has created you unique and often uses the so-called ordinary people to accomplish great things.

David wasn't even the best-liked brother in his family. His own dad didn't see him as anything but a shepherd. But God had planned something special for David. And David embraced his uniqueness and became Israel's greatest king.

Rebekah was an ordinary girl who just happened to go to the water well at the right time—the time when Abraham's servant was there in search of a wife for his master's son. Her confidence and service impressed Abraham's man, and her life was never the same. She became the wife of Isaac, one of the founding patriarchs of the Jewish people.

The men who became apostles and turned the world upside down were rather ordinary. **Peter, James, John,** and **Andrew** were rugged, uncultured fishermen. **Matthew** was a tax collector and hated by pretty much everyone in Jewish society. **Paul** was a big-time politician before he came to Christ, but many historians have said that he was short, kind of stooped over, and not very attractive.

Psalm 139:15–16 shows us that each life—your life—is valuable to God and is not an accident, but designed for His glory: *"My substance was not hid from thee when I was made in secret, and curiously wrought in the lowest parts of the earth. Thine eyes did see my substance, yet being unperfect; and in thy book all my members were written, which in continuance were fashioned, when as yet there was none of them."*

Did You Know? God didn't forget Leah. She gave birth to six sons; her fourth son, named Judah, was one of Jesus's descendants. Leah is just one of a long line of ordinary people in Jesus's family tree.

Today's Prayer: *Dear God, sometimes I feel like I'm an accident, or that I'm so ordinary that people just walk right past me. But I know You have a plan and a purpose for my life. Thank You for loving me unconditionally.*

Journal Question: How do you know that God hasn't forgotten you?

_____

_____

_____

_____

_____

_____

_____

_____

How do I handle a diva?

Today's Teen: Rachel
Today's Action Verse: Romans 12:3
Storyline: Genesis 29:1 through 30:1

Rachel Speaks Today: _"It really doesn't pay to be self-centered because it hurts not only the people closest to you; it hurts you."_

Digging Deeper: Have you ever known persons who thought they could get anything they wanted out of life? Some might call this kind of girl a diva or a prima donna. These types flaunt their money, good looks, or talents. They think they can get, and get away with, just about anything.

Rachel could have been that type of person. She was beautiful, and she knew it. She thought she was entitled to have children, just as her sister Leah had been blessed to have. She became kind of hard to deal with and made life miserable for people around her.

How do we deal with someone like this—someone who annoys or hurts us? Can a person like this ever change? The truth is that people like this can be insecure deep down and need true friendship—not a fan club. So while everyone else backstabs, gossips about, and shuns the Rachels in your church, school, or neighborhood, you can pray and take advantage of opportunities to reach their hearts, because, despite their thoughts, emotions, and actions, you know God has a plan for them.

Just Like You: Whenever Sharon's Hummer screeched into the church parking lot, all the guys and girls rolled their eyes. *Here she comes—the spoiled rich girl,* they thought. Sharon didn't exactly help herself as she prattled on about her latest shopping trips, her latest travel to Europe with her "gazillionaire" dad, and the latest celebrity she'd met (name-dropper!). It was nauseating to the rest of the girls and guys. They weren't jealous of her family's money. In fact, some of them even came from well-to-do homes, but they didn't flaunt it.

The youth group pretty much avoided Sharon until Todd, the group leader, challenged them one day. "I've got a project for 'you guys.' I want you to become Sharon's friend. I think she really is lonely and could use some true friendship—not gossipy, behind-the-back, fake friendship. How about it?" asked Todd.

Well, nobody volunteered except for Gwen—and she, reluctantly. She offered to try it for a week. She went home that night and wrote a list of things she could do to help Sharon, such as send an encouraging email, pick up the phone and call her, and maybe even go shopping with her sometimes.

Sharon is kind of annoying, but I guess everyone needs a friend, Gwen thought.

Did You Know? In Old Testament times, "men were usually the shepherds, but Laban apparently had no sons at this time, at least, none old enough to shepherd (see Genesis 29:16 and 31:1) and so it was the responsibility of his youngest daughter, Rachel, to shepherd his flock" (J. M. Freeman and H. J. Chadwick, *The New Manners & Customs of the Bible*).

Today's Prayer: *Give me the courage and strength to be a friend to the unlovable people in my world—the people who are so easy to tear down with gossip. Help me see them as You see them and love them as You do.*

Journal Question: How have you taken your insecurities out on others? How have you handled a diva? Have you responded in love? Why or why not?

_____

_____

_____

_____

_____

_____

✛ ✛ ✛ ✛ ✛ ✛ ✛ ✛ ✛ ✛ ✛ ✛ ✛ ✛ ✛ ✛ ✛

What should I do when I'm treated unfairly?

Today's Teen: Joseph
Today's Action Verse: Genesis 37:3
Storyline: Genesis 37:3–34

Joseph's Brothers Speak Today: _"When you're treated unfairly by someone you trust, leave the payback to God."_

✛ ✛

Digging Deeper: Life was dysfunctional for Joseph's brothers. Their father had four wives who constantly fought, and he was an inattentive, absentee dad. No one was in control of the house.

The worst part was the favoritism their father showed toward Joseph. Joseph was treated as though he was more special than his brothers because of who his mother was. It doesn't appear that he had to toil as much as the other brothers in the fields under the hot, summer sun. Instead, he had more freedom to roam the vast expanse of the family spread and carry messages to the other brothers. He was singled out by the father and given exceptional love and attention—which was vastly unfair to the others.

So how *should* the brothers have reacted? They were living a life they didn't choose. They were living under circumstances out of their control. And it wasn't going to change anytime soon. How *did* they react? They chose bitterness. Joseph's brothers compounded their misery by making a decision based on anger, rooted in bitter feelings, and grounded in despair. By selling their brother, Joseph, they ensured for themselves a lifetime of regret. Worse than the father's *actions* were their *reactions*.

Jealousy in the heart is like a tiny flame. If it's fed, it will grow into a raging wildfire, causing untold damage. How do you fight jealousy? How do you resist the urge to fight back? Only Jesus can give the power to love in that situation.

Just Like You: Nobody wanted the last starting position on the varsity basketball team more than Brandon did. Nobody worked harder in the off-season. Every single day, rain or shine, Brandon ran three miles, shot 200 three-pointers, and did 200 push-ups—all with one goal in mind: hearing the public address announcer introduce his name as part of the celebrated starting five before the first game of the season.

When training camp began, Brandon worked even harder. Every day, he arrived at the court a half hour early and left a half hour late. And he listened whenever Coach spoke.

Yet when the starting lineups were announced two days before the opening game, Brandon's name wasn't mentioned. Who made it instead? The coach's son had—all 135 pounds of him. Everyone knew he couldn't shoot and couldn't play defense. He couldn't even make a layup, for crying out loud! His last name was the only thing going for him. But it had been enough to land this lucky guy a spot in the coveted starting five.

That day, Brandon had a choice to make. He could drop his head, throw in the towel, and quit everything for which he had worked so hard; or he could keep plugging, keep waiting for his opportunity, and keep trusting the Lord.

Teen People of the Bible

Did You Know? Joseph's brothers hated his coat with a good reason. It was more than just a nice gift from his father; it signified their father's favoritism toward this younger brother by a different mother. Its distinct style meant he wouldn't have to work in the fields like his brothers, but would watch over them and rule from a distance.

Today's Prayer: *Lord, I don't understand why You allow me to be treated unfairly. But please show me why I can and should trust You today.*

Journal Question: How have you been treated unfairly in the last few days? How did you react? Were your reactions appropriate and pleasing to God?

_____

_____

_____

_____

_____

_____

_____

_____

_____

_____

_____

_____

_____

_____

_____

_____

DAY 22

When friends and loved ones betray me, does God really hear me?

Today's Teen: Joseph
Today's Action Verse: Genesis 37:23
Storyline: Genesis 37:23–36

Joseph Speaks Today: *"Even when your friends or family turn their backs on you, God is with you."*

✣ ✣

Digging Deeper: In a matter of moments, Joseph went from dreaming about heights of glory—where his brothers and even father, he thought, would bow down to him—to the depths of despair. He went from basking in the love of his father to experiencing cruel rejection from his brothers. He went from an exalted position to one of a common slave.

As he lay in that pit, Joseph must have realized a powerful truth that would carry him through the rest of his life. Stripped of everything he'd held dear, he had to use spiritual eyes to see that God was the only One who could help him, and God was all he needed.

When you lose everything and you're unsure if you'll survive your next breath, you suddenly see what life is all about. It's not about wealth, power, popularity, or friends; these don't help when you're at the end of your rope. When you have nothing but God—when God is all you have—you realize that God is all you need. He is the only One who can help you out of your trouble, the only port in the storm, the only sure friend.

Just Like You: Peter remembers the worst day of his life. It was a Sunday afternoon, and he was at home studying for an exam while his dad and a friend shot a round of golf. All of a sudden, the phone rang. The voice on the other end of the line was his dad's friend.

Peter looked at his watch. "Finish your round early?" he asked.

The man's tone was serious, "Pete, get your mom."

Peter yelled upstairs for his mom, she came down, and the rest of his life changed forever. His dad had collapsed just before the ninth green. The paramedics were there, but it didn't look good. Peter's father died.

Peter was 15. How could he live the rest of his life without his dad? He was his best friend. Who would he go fishing with in the summer? Who would help him with his homework? Peter would have to be the man of the house now.

God, are you there? he wondered. It was a long time before Peter prayed again. But eventually he did. His fragile faith was the only way he could muster through the grief. Peter knew God was with him, as He was with Joseph, in his pit of despair.

Did You Know? Judah was the brother whose idea it was to save Joseph's life and sell him into slavery. It would be through Judah's bloodline that the Messiah, Jesus, would eventually be born.

Today's Prayer: *Lord, sometimes You allow things to happen that I don't understand. But I know I can trust You when my world falls apart.*

Journal Question: Sometimes it may seem as though God doesn't hear your prayers. How can you be sure that He does?

_____

_____

_____

_____

_____

_____

_____

DAY 23

How can I make something good out of the bad situations in life?

Today's Teen: Joseph
Today's Action Verse: Genesis 39:2
Storyline: Genesis 39:1–6

Joseph Speaks Today: *"When bad things happen, you can give up in fear, or you can trust God and make the best of it."*

Digging Deeper: With every mile of bumpy road from Canaan to Egypt, Joseph must have pondered his future. It was the longest journey of his life. So unexpected! So out of his control! Something had gone terribly wrong between him and his brothers.

But what choice did Joseph have? He could sulk, or he could look to God for strength. Remember that Joseph did not know what was going to happen next. All he knew was that he would be a slave in a foreign land. Who and where would he serve? What kind of work would he have to do? Where would he sleep? What would he eat? Would he ever get to go back home?

What do you do when life suddenly takes a wrong turn? Who do you lean on for support when a parent walks out, a loved one dies, or a friend turns on you?

You have a choice. You can grow bitter, or you can look to God for strength to make the best of a bad situation.

Teen People of the Bible

Just Like You: At 17, Joni Eareckson Tada had everything ahead of her: college, relationships, and a singing career. Then, on one ordinary summer day, she lost it all in a terrible diving accident. The doctors told her she would never walk again and never be able to use her hands again. In a matter of hours, life turned from hopeful to hopeless. Who would marry her? Who would hire her? Could she go to college?

That was in 1967. Today, Joni is still a quadriplegic, but her life has touched millions. Her beautiful portraits, created painstakingly by placing a paintbrush between her teeth, are highly sought after. She's an award-winning gospel singer and the host of a radio program, *Joni and Friends.* Joni has also served on presidential commissions, has founded an organization that ministers to those with disabilities, and is a popular speaker at churches, retreats, and conferences. Joni's life could have been over after her accident. But Joni realized, as did Joseph after many years, that God's best purposes are often found after our best plans are shattered.

Did You Know? Slavery might seem to you like an outdated practice, but unfortunately, it's alive and well today—only now it's more commonly referred to as *human trafficking.* Young girls and boys from underdeveloped countries are sold as property to wealthy businesses that employ these innocent people as sex slaves.

Today's Prayer: *Lord, I'm not quite sure where You are leading me in my life, and I'm not so sure I'll always like it, but please help me always to make the best of my situation.*

Journal Question: Why do you sometimes feel like life is hopeless? How can you make the best out of those situations?

_____

_____

_____

_____

_____

_____

DAY 24

Is it possible to resist sexual temptation?

Today's Teen: Joseph
Today's Action Verses: Genesis 39:8–9
Storyline: Genesis 39:7–23

Joseph Speaks Today: *"Saying yes to sexual purity isn't easy, but it is always the best choice."*

Digging Deeper: Joseph had every excuse to say yes to this powerful woman, Potiphar's wife. He was away from home. Everyone had abandoned him. I imagine people around him said, "C'mon, Joseph, you deserve this."

But Joseph resisted. Why?

Here is my take on it: First of all, God was with Joseph. Secondly, Joseph was a respectful guy and loyal to his master. Joseph's physical purity began with his spiritual purity and daily walk with God. Thirdly, Joseph knew the difference between lust and love. By keeping himself pure, he would experience all the best that God had to offer. He knew having sex with a woman who was not his wife would be dishonoring to God. Accepting a cheap and unfulfilling substitute for God's best went against everything he believed.

Joseph succeeded in a culture that celebrated sin, not because he was a spiritual giant, but, I say, because he determined early on to keep his purity. His decision to resist temptation began in his soul.

Just Like You: An "Ask Amy" column in the *Chicago Tribune* began like this: "I am a 15-year-old girl and a freshman in high school. I take pride in the fact that I am a virgin and that I plan to—and can—wait until marriage. All of my friends know this, and all of them respect me for it. Life without that worry has been great."

She went on to say how worried she was about a friend who had not made the same decision. This courageous teen is a modern-day Joseph in her school. The choice she made can be a hard choice, because pressure comes daily from numerous directions: friends and popular culture. But in resisting the temptation and choosing to follow God, she'll avoid the consequences that come with a sexual relationship outside the boundaries of marriage. She'll be able to give her future husband a priceless gift: the gift of purity. Unlike most of her peers, this girl understands that God's boundaries were not given to take away our joy, but were actually designed to maximize our joy.

Did You Know? Best-selling author Randy Alcorn has this to say in his book, *The Purity Principle*: "God's guardrails are His moral laws. They stand between us and destruction. They are there not to punish or deprive us, but to protect us."

Today's Prayer: *Lord, sometimes I feel too weak to resist temptation. Please give me the strength to stay pure in all that I do.*

Journal Question: Why is it so hard to resist sexual temptation? What can you do to arm yourself against such a compelling enemy?

_____

_____

_____

_____

_____

_____

_____

_____

Why does God allow evil things to happen to good people?

Today's Teen: Joseph
Today's Action Verse: Genesis 39:21
Storyline: Genesis 39:7–23; Genesis 40

Joseph Speaks Today: *"When you don't really understand what God is doing, hang in there, because eventually, He'll work things out in your favor."*

Digging Deeper: If you were Joseph, sitting in a filthy Egyptian dungeon, how close would you be to quitting on the whole idea of trusting God?

Could Joseph's life sink any lower? Egypt wasn't like America. There were no appeals, no hunger strikes outside the prison, no Court TV lawyers pleading his case. This was Egypt, ruled by a powerful Pharaoh. Potiphar, the guy Joseph worked for, was a big-time politician. Joseph had no legal recourse. He had no way out. But God wanted him right there in that prison because He had a most amazing plan.

Maybe you're going through a tough time and you don't understand how God can let it happen. But Scripture teaches that God sometimes allows sickness, loss, injustice, and tragedy to shape us, prove us, and make us into better persons. Just as Joseph's time in prison shaped his character, so your trials will shape you.

Just Like You: Jenny was a Christian and the captain of the varsity volleyball team. She tried to let her faith show in the way she treated people rather than putting it in their faces. One day, she was invited to a party at a teammate's house. Someone told her alcohol would be served. Jenny said politely that she couldn't go, and thought that was the end of it.

The day after the big party, Jenny saw three of her teammates being ushered into the coach's office. Later, she found out they had been kicked off the team. The coach had found out about the party. After a few days, a rumor spread around school that Jenny had tattled to the coach about the party so she could get more playing time. It wasn't true, of course, but that didn't matter. Soon it seemed that all the girls refused to talk to her. All she did was do the right thing—quietly, discreetly, and gently—yet her motives were being called into question.

Jenny began to second-guess herself: *Maybe I should have gone to the party. Maybe I shouldn't have said anything.* Did Jenny do the right thing?

Sometimes you'll do the right thing and have your motives questioned. It's hard to take, but it often comes with the territory. But take heart, because Jesus, who was perfect, was wrongly accused and was crucified for it. He knows your pain.

Did You Know? Author Ray Pritchard, in his book, *Keep Believing,* says, "We gain more from sickness than we do from health. We pray more when we are scared than when we are confident. And everything that happens to you—the tragedies, the unexplained circumstances, even the stupid choices you make—all of it is grist for the mill of God's loving purpose."

Today's Prayer: *Lord, I know You were treated unfairly at the cross, when You had to take the blame for my sins. Please help me in times when I'm unfairly accused.*

Journal Question: Who are some of the "good people" who seem to have been singled out for trials? What were the results?

_____

_____

_____

_____

_____

DAY 26

Why does God wait so long to answer my prayers?

Today's Teen: Joseph
Today's Action Verse: Genesis 41:41
Storyline: Genesis 41

Joseph Speaks Today: *"Waiting is really no fun, but it doesn't mean that God has forgotten you—only that His timing is slightly different than yours."*

Digging Deeper: Nobody likes to wait, whether standing in a long grocery line, sitting in traffic, or anticipating an important phone call. Joseph was no different. Sure he became a leader in prison and won the hearts of important people. But come on! *He was still in prison for a crime he didn't commit.*

God waited a long time—in our eyes—to change Joseph's life. Joseph experienced years of uncertainty. But you'll notice the Bible says God was *with* Joseph (Acts 7:9). This prison sentence was no accident. God was preparing Joseph for something greater, but Joseph didn't know that. In fact, he had no idea if he'd ever get out of prison. But he had had two dreams.

Why doesn't God act when it seems we need Him the most? Why doesn't He routinely put families back together? Why doesn't He miraculously cure every cancer? Why doesn't He send money down from heaven?

Waiting forces us to our knees. It sets our hurried clocks to God's unrushed calendar. When we wait, we realize we are helpless without God and completely dependent on His power and strength.

It is in those awful, agonizing weeks, months, or, often, years of uncertainty that we really discover who God is and who we are.

Just Like You: Amy really wishes she could have a godly boyfriend who could one day be her husband. Other girls in her youth group have boyfriends, but no guy in the group has ever expressed interest in her. And now she's a senior in high school.

Amy knows she is still very young and that God may have someone special for her in college, but it is still hard to wait. She has days in which she looks in the mirror and feels unattractive.

Several boys at her school like her, but she knows they are not serious about following the Lord.

Waiting is hard—whether it's Joseph, waiting for a get-out-of-jail-free card, or Amy, hoping silently for someone to love her. We often get discouraged and think God is ignoring our needs or punishing us for some reason. But that's not true; He operates on a different timetable than we do. We need to trust that He is in control even while we are waiting.

Did You Know? Ancient Egypt was one of the most advanced civilizations in history. Paintings preserved in pyramids for thousands of years share vivid stories of complex brain surgeries, detailed building blueprints, running water, and other things. So Joseph's long wait ended in promotion to second in command of a very classy country.

Today's Prayer: *Lord, I want everything to happen according to my own timing, but Your timing is so much better. Help me to understand this and not quit trusting when it seems You have forgotten to answer my prayer.*

Journal Question: What are some of your unanswered prayers that you still want God to answer?

_____

_____

_____

_____

_____

DAY 27

Can a young person really make a difference?

Today's Teen: Miriam
Today's Action Verse: 1 Timothy 4:12
Storyline: Exodus 2:1–10

Miriam Speaks Today: *"If you can do something to change someone's life, don't be afraid to speak up. God can give you the words to say."*

Digging Deeper: Most historians believe Miriam was in her teens when she stood by the bank of the Nile and watched over her baby brother, Moses. She, having helped her family hide a male baby, could easily have been caught or killed for going against Pharaoh's orders. Miriam was not only loyal to her family but also wise to offer her mom as a caregiver for Moses. Miriam's quick thinking not only saved her brother but saved a nation, for it would be Moses who would one day lead the children of Israel out of Egyptian bondage.

Like Miriam, you might someday be called upon to save someone in need. You might have an opportunity to share your faith with a friend or relative. Or maybe you'll have to rescue someone in danger. Clear thinking may help diffuse a crisis at school, at home, or in the neighborhood.

In whatever way God leads you, you can be sure He will give you, as He did Miriam, the courage and strength to act quickly and do the right thing.

Just Like You: Robert had recently made it a private goal to share his faith with at least one person every month. One day Robert and his dad went to see their favorite baseball team. They had front-row tickets behind the home-team dugout. Robert was excited.

In the second inning, two guys came and sat next to him. After a few minutes, Robert struck up a conversation. They talked about the game and their favorite players. One of the guys noticed Robert's T-shirt. On the front were the words *Fear Not.*

Robert explained that the words were from the Bible. Looks of discomfort washed across their faces.

"Wait a minute," Robert said, as he proceeded to tell them his journey of faith.

He told them how he had always had fear—fear of the unknown, fear of relationships, fear of what he would encounter when he went off to college. He stated that one day he was invited to a youth event at a nearby church, where he heard about Jesus, who takes away fear. He continued by saying that since then, since he trusted in Christ as his Savior, he knows what to do with any fear that comes his way. Whenever he starts growing fearful, he takes it to God and just trusts Him.

The guys seemed interested, but Robert didn't press them. He got their email addresses and promised to send more information. Then he whispered a prayer: *Thank You for giving me the courage to talk to these guys about faith.* He knew God had put him in this position to plant a seed of faith.

Did You Know? Miriam grew to be a leader among the children of Israel. She also became a musician who created beautiful songs. Her most popular song was written after God opened the Red Sea and allowed His chosen people to walk through on dry land (Exodus 15:20–21).

Today's Prayer: *God, please give me the courage and wisdom to speak up when You provide me an opportunity.*

Journal Question: What can you do today to make a difference in your church, at your school, or among your group of friends?

_____

_____

_____

_____

DAY 28

Can God use me in spite of where I came from?

Today's Teen: Moses

Today's Action Verses: 1 Corinthians 1:26–29

Storyline: Acts 7:17–22

Moses Speaks Today: *"It doesn't matter what family, what cultural group, or what background you come from, because God can take you anywhere."*

Digging Deeper: Moses's life is the original rags-to-riches story. Hollywood couldn't have scripted it better. God brought Moses from the slimy mud of the Nile to the royal halls of Egypt, the world's superpower. Moses lived in the house of the most powerful man in the world. He was educated at the best schools and surrounded by wealth and privilege.

The life of Moses is a perfect example of God's love. Born into the lowest race in Egypt, Moses had no business walking the halls of royalty. Yet God wanted him there, and God put him there. Moses's life is proof that God can work out His plan for anyone, regardless of his or her circumstances.

The world classifies people by race, class, or education, but *"God is no respecter of persons"* (Acts 10:34). Don't let anyone tell you that your background, race, or gender will keep you from achieving all that God wills for your life. Who you are or where you came from doesn't matter—only where you are going.

Just Like You: Condoleezza Rice may be one of the most powerful women in the world. She was a trusted advisor to two presidents and rose to the key position of Secretary of State. But in the 1950s in Birmingham, Alabama, nobody would have dreamed that an African American woman could get so far. Born in Birmingham, Condoleezza grew up in what was a hotbed of racism, where ugly Jim Crow laws kept African American people from having equal opportunities. They were often denied service at restaurants and department stores. They lived under constant threat of abuse and death.

One day, while Condi and her family were worshipping at her father's church, a bomb exploded two blocks away at the Sixteenth Street Baptist Church, killing four girls, one of whom was Condoleezza's classmate.

Condi's father, a preacher, instilled in her the value of hard work, faith, and confidence. He often told her she could do whatever the Lord wanted her to do, despite the odds. Those principles have guided Condi her entire life.

Because she didn't allow her early setbacks to keep her from success, Condoleezza Rice became one of the most powerful and influential women in American history (Sheryl Henderson Blunt, "The Unflappable Condi Rice," *Christianity Today,* September 2003).

Did You Know? Historian Alfred Edersheim talks about education in ancient Egypt: "Education was carried to a very great length, and, in the case of those destined for the higher professions, embraced not only the various sciences, as mathematics, astronomy, chemistry, medicine, etc., but theology, philosophy, and a knowledge of the laws. There can be no doubt that, as the adopted son of the princess, Moses would receive the highest training."

Today's Prayer: *Dear Lord, I don't know what Your plan is for my life, but I do know that You can take me where I am and use me for Your glory.*

Journal Question: How can you find relief when the ugliness of your past haunts you?

DAY 29

Is it important to remember my roots?

Today's Teen: Moses
Today's Action Verse: Esther 4:14
Storyline: Acts 7:20–25

Moses Speaks Today: *"Don't let anyone convince you to abandon your faith, because it will carry you through the tough choices of life."*

Digging Deeper: As the son of Pharaoh's daughter and possibly future Pharaoh, Moses was brought up in the culture and lifestyle of Egypt, one of the most advanced societies in the history of the world. He was living far removed from the poverty and pain of his Hebrew family.

Even though Moses looked, sounded, and dressed like a royal Egyptian, he was still a Hebrew at heart. The fame and fortune of his position didn't keep him from remembering his roots. His foundation of faith kept him humble, and God raised him up to deliver God's people from bondage and bring Him glory.

Similarly, God has put you in a special place to fulfill His will; but you, like Moses, will be tempted to abandon everything you've known. People will pressure you to forsake your childhood values, to give up your faith, and become a man or woman of the world. But if you stay true to your roots, you'll understand you were born in this time and place for a purpose—to influence this generation for Christ.

Just Like You: Even though Katie grew up in a broken home, her mother always took her to church and faithfully taught her the importance of a daily relationship with God through prayer and Bible reading. Katie's mom often told her, "I feel like God has something special for your life," and Katie believed she would be a missionary or pastor's wife one day.

When Katie went off to college, she started hanging with some friends who questioned her beliefs. Thoughts like, *How do you know Christianity is the only way to God?* and *How do you know the Bible is even true?* bombarded her mind daily. She faced not only hostility from her friends but also ridicule and scorn from her liberal teachers.

The questions took a toll, planting seeds of doubt in Katie's mind. When she went home for Christmas break, her mom noticed a difference: Katie wasn't as eager to get up for church on Sunday morning. She stopped listening to praise songs in the car. And she seemed to have lost her passion for sharing her faith.

At first, Katie's mom kept quiet about what she noticed. But a few weeks after the break, she wrote a letter to Katie. After expressing her love for Katie and hopes for another good semester, she wrote, "Katie, please don't forget your roots. Stay grounded in God's Word. That's where your strength lies."

Did You Know? The Pharaohs of ancient Egypt were obsessed with the afterlife. As soon as they came to the throne, they began working on their tombs—the pyramids that still dot the landscape of this Middle Eastern country. The pyramids were often filled with the most ornate gold and jewels, detailed carvings, chariots, battle equipment, and even boats. Sometimes the Pharaohs would be buried with their servants. All this was in futile preparation for their version of everlasting life.

Today's Prayer: *Dear God, help me never forget why You brought me into this world—and that is, to glorify You. Keep me strongly anchored to my faith roots.*

Journal Question: Do you feel tempted to abandon any part of your faith?

_____

_____

_____

_____

_____

Is it a mistake to give up something important for God?

Today's Teen: Moses
Today's Action Verse: Matthew 16:24
Storyline: Hebrews 11:23–27

Moses Speaks Today: *"Fame and fortune are fleeting, but a life of radical devotion to Christ brings ultimate satisfaction."*

Digging Deeper: In the opinion of his friends and relatives, Moses made a foolish decision. Why would he give up a life of money, parties, and power to live among the Hebrews who were the lowest class in Egypt? How could Moses refuse the opportunity to run the world's most powerful country?

My thought is that Moses wasn't satisfied with a mediocre walk with God, and he knew that his comfortable life in the palace would keep him from experiencing the fullness of God's perfect will.

Sometimes we're called to sacrifice things we desire because they get between God and us. It could be something completely harmless, like a relationship, a job offer, or even a hobby or sport. Hebrews 12:1 calls these unnecessary things *weights*: *"Let us lay aside every weight, and the sin which doth so easily beset us, and let us run with patience the race that is set before us."* Think of a marathon runner who dresses as light as he can to win the race.

Jesus calls us to an extreme faith—extreme trust in God—even to the point of self-denial (Matthew 16:24). He calls us to make a choice between comfortable faith and radical discipleship. We know which one Moses chose. What about you?

Teen People of the Bible

Just Like You: When quarterback, Danny Wuerffel, a former Heisman Trophy winner, retired from the NFL, he had his pick of lucrative opportunities in broadcasting, coaching, and business. But instead, Wuerffel chose to become development director of Desire Street Ministries, a ministry for young troubled teens in the heart of New Orleans' Lower Ninth Ward. This crime-ridden section of the inner city is one of the most impoverished areas of the country.

"If I had five lives to live, I'd do a lot of different things," says Danny, "but when you have one life, you have to choose very carefully" (Gail Wood, "Danny Wuerffel Finds Hope After Katrina," *Breakaway,* 2005).

Like Moses, Danny had to make a choice that wasn't exactly easy. In 2005, the waters of Katrina completely destroyed Danny's home and the Desire Street Ministries' buildings. But Danny has remained committed to the task, temporarily moving the ministries to Baton Rouge and planning the ministries' comeback to the same impoverished area of New Orleans.

Danny Wuerffel is committed to using his money, influence, and talents for God's glory.

Did You Know? Some historians believe that Moses was next in line to be Pharaoh, not only because he was gifted, handsome, and well-liked, but because he may have been the only, though adopted, heir to the throne. The historian Josephus said that Moses's adoptive mother didn't have any sons and thought of Moses as a gift from the gods.

Today's Prayer: *Dear Lord, help me to make choices based on eternity, rather than this present world. Help me to see beyond the glitz and glamour of the world.*

Journal Question: What sacrifices have you made to follow God? How did you feel after you made those tough choices?

_____

_____

_____

_____

_____

DAY 31

How can I help those who are less fortunate?

Today's Teen: Moses
Today's Action Verse: Matthew 9:36
Storyline: Exodus 2:11

Moses Speaks Today: *"You can always do something to help the less fortunate."*

✚ ✚

Digging Deeper: Every time Moses heard the sharp crack of a whip hitting the raw flesh of a Hebrew slave, he felt his own heart pierced with pain, I imagine. *Can't I do something?* he must have wondered.

Moses couldn't bear to watch his people suffer under the cruel thumb of an evil ruler. Even though he lived in luxury and had access to the perks of royal life, his young heart was tender to the needs of the Hebrews, who were so much less fortunate. He desperately wanted to do something—anything—to rescue them from their pain.

Just as it would have been easy for Moses to turn away from the suffering of the Hebrew slaves, it's also easy for Americans to ignore the needs of the less fortunate in our communities and around the world.

You may not be in a position of power as Moses was, and you certainly wouldn't want to choose a solution like the one he chose in Exodus 2:12, but there is always something positive you can do, something you can give. It may be as simple as doing some yard work for an elderly widow, volunteering at a homeless shelter over the holidays, or helping a sick family clean their house. If your heart is sensitive to the needs of others, you'll be motivated to do what you can to make their lives better.

Just Like You: Elizabeth was at home sick and flipping through channels. She stumbled across a news channel that was broadcasting a documentary on the crisis in the Sudan. Outside of civics and history, Elizabeth had never really paid much attention to what went on over there. She felt as if God had given her so much to do here at home, there was little she could do for people thousands of miles away. But the TV kept flashing images of starving young kids, many of whom were born with HIV/AIDS. She tried to change the channel, but the images kept haunting her. She went back and watched the documentary until the very end. When it was over, she felt God speaking to her heart: *Do something.* But what could she do?

Later that week, she mentioned her experience to a couple of her Christian friends. One of them told her about a special missions trip the church was taking to Africa. The group was leaving in four months and was looking for a few more volunteers to help pass out food and supplies in one of the continent's worst areas. "Maybe we could go," another friend offered.

After talking it over with their parents, Elizabeth and her friends each decided to take the leap of faith. They would work odd jobs all summer to raise enough money for the trip. And they would write letters to friends and relatives asking for support. They knew they couldn't save a whole continent, but they could *do something.*

Did You Know? Most of the pyramids in Egypt were built with granite stone. But in the last few years, archaeologists have discovered pyramids made with mud bricks, possibly from the time of the Hebrews.

Today's Prayer: *Dear Lord, please give me a tender heart toward the poor, the needy, and the unsaved.*

Journal Question: Who are some of the less fortunate in your community? In what ways could you help them?

_____

_____

_____

_____

_____

DAY 32

Can a harlot come to faith?

Today's Teen: Rahab
Today's Action Verse: Hebrews 11:31
Storyline: Joshua 2

Rahab Speaks Today: *"Even as a harlot, I could recognize a God thing when I saw it. I acted on my belief, and God changed me and gave me a future."*

Digging Deeper: Of all the people who could have been spared from Jericho's destruction, why did God choose Rahab, who either was a prostitute or among the low-class innkeepers? Either way, her standing in society was low. Why did God *not* choose to spare an artist or scientist or athlete *instead*—someone who could bring value to Israel's future?

The answer is simple and yet profound. It's what separates Christianity from every other religion. It's this concept called *grace*.

This same grace sent Jesus to earth to give His life so prostitutes, drug dealers, murderers, cheaters, liars, and gossipers could find restoration and hope in a relationship with their Creator.

You may be thinking thoughts like these: *Yeah right, but you don't know what I've done. You don't know where I've been. You don't know what choices I've made.*

No, I don't know. But God knows, and He loves you anyway. Not for what you can offer Him, but because He created you for a purpose.

Rahab's story can be your story. Her scarlet cord protected her from God's wrath on Jericho, and Christ's blood can protect you from the wrath of God upon sin. Forgiveness has been provided *for you!*

Rahab acknowledged God and His work, and God saved her. What about you? Seek Him and discover Someone who loves you unconditionally.

Just Like You: Percy Edmonds grew up in a good home, in a Christian family, in a western suburb of Chicago. He seemed to have everything going for him. He was a track and football star and got good grades in school.

But as Percy grew older, he grew restless. He stopped going to church and was kicked out of the Christian school he attended. It wasn't long before he joined a street gang and starting using drugs.

At the age of 16, Percy landed in jail. He was paroled but was incarcerated two months later on another charge. There in his jail cell, Percy threw his hands up and prayed to God, "God, I've had enough of my own way. Please help me." Immediately Bible verses came to his mind—verses he'd memorized in church and school.

Percy threw himself into God's Word, joining a jail Bible study, attending sanctioned church retreats, and eventually leading others to Christ.

One day, Percy got some good news. He would be released.

When out, he, in time, found his way to the historic Pacific Garden Mission in Chicago, where he enrolled in the Bible program. Percy Edmonds is now attending Dayspring Bible College and Seminary and plans on serving in the ministry full-time.

Did You Know? Rahab became the wife of Salmon, a prince of the tribe of Judah. Her great-great-grandson was David, the king of Israel. And so Rahab, the prostitute, became an ancestor to Jesus Christ, the promised Messiah. How about that!

Today's Prayer: *Dear God, thank You for loving me, despite what I've done. I want to grab hold of Your love. I want Your power to change my life; I want to let Your glory shine through me. Thank You for Your unmatched grace.*

Journal Question: Most people put conditions on their love. How does God's love for you differ, and how does that make you feel?

_____

_____

_____

_____

_____

_____

DAY 33

What if I have to lie to protect someone's life?

Today's Teen: Rahab
Today's Action Verses: Joshua 2:4–6
Storyline: Joshua 2

Rahab Speaks Today: *"Faith in God often causes you to have to make tough choices."*

✤ ❖ ✤ ✤ ✤ ✤ ✤ ✤ ❖ ✤ ✤ ✤ ✤ ✤ ❖ ✤ ✤ ✤ ✤ ✤ ❖ ✧

Digging Deeper: This passage holds many truths for living. One question that arises when looking at it is this: Was it right for Rahab to lie? Parents, teachers, coaches, or anyone else who has influence in our lives usually will tell us that it's never right to lie.

What about the moral dilemma Rahab faced? She could tell the truth to the Jericho "police," the messengers from the king, and sell out the spies, or she could lie and ensure their safety. If she told the truth, the plan for the children of Israel to conquer Jericho might have been compromised. Ultimately, Rahab made the right choice to trust the God who had demonstrated His power in behalf of the children of Israel. She aligned herself with God's people, as is evident from the outcome—Rahab believed in the Lord, and her household was saved as a result of her actions. But she lied.

Teen People of the Bible

Rahab wasn't the only person in the Bible who had to make that type of choice. The Hebrew nurses in Egypt lied to Pharaoh to save Hebrew boys from infanticide (Exodus 1:15–22). To avoid the wrath of Saul, Samuel spoke per God's instruction, telling only part of the mission when he went to anoint David to be Israel's second king (1 Samuel 16:1–5). Some might term that a half-truth, same as a lie.

However, these accounts in the Bible do not give you license for willy-nilly lying to parents, teachers, or coaches. Rarely will you ever be forced to break a rule for a good purpose. But in those times when you are faced with a moral dilemma, you can look to Rahab and other characters in the Bible as examples of persons who did the right thing in God's eyes.

God understands the tough choices you sometimes have to make. He understands the nitty-gritty of life in a fallen world.

Just Like You: So is it ever right to lie? What if you're in a situation similar to Rahab's and you're forced to choose between two morals—for example, lying and loyalty to God? Here are some important points to remember:

- **Make sure you're really in a tough spot.** Don't use Rahab's experience as a license to lie. Most of the time, there is no reason to lie in order to obey God's laws.
- **If you are sure you're being faced with a tough moral choice, always choose the "higher moral."** For instance, if by withholding an unnecessary truth, you save someone from being hurt, then you may not want to voice that truth. Again, go with the higher moral. In Rahab's case, lying was a choice she made to avoid risking the lives of the spies.
- **Pray for God's guidance.** You can be sure that God understands your dilemma and knows what's at stake. Don't be afraid to approach Him and ask for help and wisdom.
- **Make sure your objective is spiritual.** Don't lie just for the sake of convenience. Something big must be at stake, like someone's life.
- **Don't rejoice in breaking a law.** You never see Rahab gloat about lying to the king's messengers. I'd like to believe that she wished she could have done it another way. Boasting about lying or breaking rules only reveals a deeper problem of rebellion and lack of respect for God.

Did You Know? Why did Rahab have stalks of flax on her roof? In those days, flax was used to make linen and yarn and was often set out on the roof to dry.

Today's Prayer: *Dear God, when I'm faced with a moral dilemma, like Rahab was, please give me wisdom to make the right choice.*

Journal Question: What would you have done if you had been in Rahab's position?

_____

_____

_____

_____

✛ ✛ ✛ ✛ ✛ ✛ ✛ ✛ ✛   ✛ ✛ ✛ ✛ ✛ ✛ ✛ ✛ ✛

What happens if I waste my talents?

Today's Teen: Samson
Today's Action Verse: Judges 13:5
Storyline: Judges 13–16

Samson Speaks Today: *"Physical strength without spiritual strength is useless—because the latter is what will carry you through life."*

✛ ✛ ✛ ✛ ✛ ✛ ✛ ✛ ✛ ✛ ✛ ✛ ✛ ✛ ✛ ✛ ✛ ✛ ✛

Digging Deeper: When you think about Samson, you probably think of the world's strongest man, a comic-book figure, a superhero, such as Superman, Spider-Man, Batman, or the Hulk. But Bible teacher Warren Wiersbe writes a sad, but true, commentary about Samson:

Samson illustrates people who have power to conquer others, but who cannot conquer themselves. He set the Philistine fields on fire, but could not control the fires of his own lust. He killed a lion, but would not put to death the passions of the flesh. He could easily break the bonds that men put on him, but the shackles of sin gradually grew stronger on his soul. Instead of leading the nation, he preferred to work independently, and as a result, left no permanent victory behind. He was remembered for what he destroyed, not for what he built up.

—Warren W. Wiersbe, *Wiersbe's Expository Outlines on the Old Testament* ✝

You can be a spiritual giant by admitting your weakness and depending upon God's strength to carry you through life.

Just Like You: God had given Doug some special gifts—that was obvious, even in his early years. He was an accomplished pianist, he had a beautiful singing voice, and everyone at school loved him. Most people felt Doug would have a huge impact on the world for Christ. But early during Doug's senior year of high school, he began slipping in his spiritual walk. He stopped reading his Bible, started hanging out with some questionable friends in the neighborhood, and began seeing a certain girl, even knowing his parents didn't approve of her.

Worried by these signs, Doug's parents talked to him about his choices. They tried not to be too harsh, but Doug took their mild rebukes as simply another example of their attempts, along with those of the church, to control his life. *Why can't I be what I want to be? Does everyone have to tell me what to do?* he thought.

Doug continued to go his own way. By the end of his senior year, Doug dropped out of school. Then one day, Doug grabbed all his belongings and moved out of the house. Rumor had it that he was going to move in with his girlfriend. Over the next few years, Doug continued to make tragic choices. He moved from state to state. He lost his money and had to sleep in his car and at friends' homes. He started drinking and using drugs. Then, five years after high school, Doug was found dead of an overdose. At his funeral, his parents, Christian friends, and his pastor—everyone who knew him—wept at Doug's shortened life and wondered what went wrong.

Did You Know? The angel of the Lord told Samson's mom that, though she had been barren until that time, she would have a son, so she was *not* to drink alcohol or eat anything unclean. The angel gave Samson's parents some further instructions and information about their coming son: No razor should come on his head, for he was to be a Nazirite unto God *from birth;* and he would begin to free Israel from the control of the Philistines.

A Nazirite was not allowed to have a haircut, drink alcohol, or come near a dead body. The purpose of the vow of the Nazirite was to separate a person unto the Lord. Samson was to be separated to the Lord from the time of his birth for a specific purpose—to begin freeing Israel.

Today's Prayer: *Dear God, please help me to use my talents and gifts for You. I know that You are the One who gave me my abilities and that You are the Source of my strength.*

Journal Question: In what ways can you surrender your gifts to God's glory today?

_____

_____

_____

_____

_____

_____

_____

_____

_____

_____

_____

_____

_____

DAY 35

What is the big deal about my spiritual heritage?

Today's Teen: Samson
Today's Action Verse: Ephesians 6:1
Storyline: Judges 14

Samson Speaks Today: *"Don't carelessly toss away your upbringing, because it's a strong foundation on which to lean. It's a guide for important decisions in your future."*

Digging Deeper: Like many young people, Samson grew up in a godly home. He learned to walk with God from an early age and knew right from wrong. He had a priceless treasure: a spiritual heritage.

But instead of embracing the faith of his parents, Samson seemed determined to chuck everything he knew in favor of the so-called good life. Maybe he felt cheated—confined within the boundaries of his parents' faith. His eyes longed for the pleasures of the world.

Perhaps you feel a little like Samson—too confined inside the tight walls of your parents' faith. You think, *Why all the rules? Why can't I have any fun?*

If you are feeling that way—it's OK. It's natural to question why and what you're doing. But don't let those questions take you down Samson's rocky path—his was a life lived away from the protective umbrella of God's will. Your Christian heritage is a great treasure. Seek the good in it.

Just Like You: The Bible has a lot to say about honoring and obeying your parents (Exodus 20:12; Ephesians 6:1). But what does this mean? Does this mean you have to agree with everything they say or do? No. Here is what it really means to honor your parents:

- **Always treat them with respect and dignity.** Despite your parents' weaknesses and shortcomings (you have weaknesses and shortcomings too, you know), God wants you to treat them with dignity and respect. Even if your parents aren't believers, you should treat them well.
- **Try not to say anything hurtful that you might regret later.** When you're in a disagreement with your mom or dad, it is very easy to get upset with them and say something very hurtful. But as soon as the ugly words come out, you'll likely feel terribly. It's better to hold your tongue and ask God to change your heart.
- **Obey your parents' rules of the house.** This is a hard one. Maybe your friends get away with disregarding their parents, but God expects you, a Christian, to obey your parents' rules as long as you live in their home. When you leave, you can set up your own boundaries. But they are your parents, and God commands you to honor them. And, if they're footing the bill for everything, they have a right to make the rules.
- **Follow in your parents' faith.** This doesn't mean you have to practice your faith exactly like your parents practice theirs. But if you walk with God, this is the greatest gift you can give Christian parents. You surely can ask and receive priceless advice on spiritual matters.
- **Don't talk down your parents behind their backs.** It's so tempting to dump on your mom and dad when you're in the locker room or on the phone with your friends, but God hates gossip and put-downs—especially about your parents.

Did You Know? In the Old Testament, believers didn't have the blessing of the Holy Spirit, except when anointed or chosen for special callings. Samson was one of those especially equipped by the Spirit of the Lord (Judges 13:25; 14:19; 15:14). Today, all believers are given the Holy Spirit when they become a Christian.

Today's Prayer: *Dear God, help me to honor my parents and obey them, even when I really don't agree and really don't feel like doing it.*

Journal Question: What can you do to honor your parents, even if they seem a little overprotective?

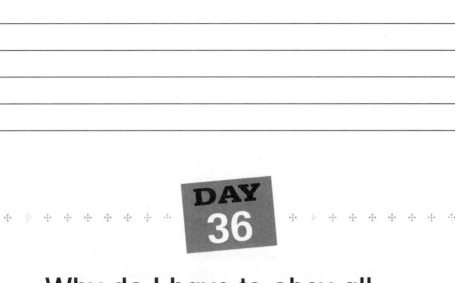

Why do I have to obey all the rules?

Today's Teen: Samson
Today's Action Verse: Hebrews 13:7
Storyline: Judges 14–16

Samson Speaks Today: *"The life of a rebel is hard—full of trouble and a miserable journey away from the God who loves us."*

Digging Deeper: Samson, in my opinion, was the poster child for rebellion. He defied every level of authority in his life, from his parents to the laws of the land to the special vow God had called him to. Basically, Samson didn't seem to care what the rules were; he was going to do what he wanted to do.

Samson seemed to get away with his behavior for quite a while. But Samson eventually had to face the consequences of his actions—consequences such as misery, bad relationships, and an enemy that wanted to kill him. Worst of all, he had walked all over God's laws and was out of the umbrella of God's protection.

Samson's cocky, who-cares attitude got him nowhere, and that kind of attitude will get you nowhere. It's better to obey the authority God has put in your life, even if it seems kind of lame. If you're rebelling against your parents, teachers, and coaches, you're really fighting God.

Just Like You: Why is it such a big deal to obey authority? The Apostle Paul shared an incredible truth with the early church, which was struggling to obey an ungodly government: *"There is no power but of God: the powers that be are ordained of God"* (Romans 13:1). This includes all authority, whether Christian or not.

However, on rare occasion, persons have had to *disobey* authority to *obey* God. Here are some examples from the Bible and modern history:

- **Peter** and the other apostles refused to stop preaching the gospel when the civil authorities told them they must stop (Acts 5:29).
- When **Rahab** hid the spies who came from among the children of Israel to check out the land, she lied to the men the king had sent to look for them (Joshua 2).
- The **nurses in Egypt** refused to kill the Hebrew boy babies and lied to the Pharaoh about it (Exodus 1:19).
- In the 1940s during the Holocaust, young **Corrie ten Boom** in Holland lied to the Nazi guards when they asked if her family was hiding Jewish people (*The Hiding Place*).
- **Martin Luther King Jr.** and the leaders of the civil rights movement peacefully protested the racist laws and policies in America.

Did You Know? We often think of Samson as being way bigger than most guys his age—kind of like Goliath. But Samson was likely no bigger than the average guy. It was his strength that was so unusual. He probably looked normal until he did something wild—like picking up a city gate!

Today's Prayer: *God, help me obey my parents, my teachers, my coaches, and everyone You have put in authority over me—unless doing so goes against what I know Your will to be. I know obedience to authority is the best way—Your way to success.*

Journal Question: Why does it seem so hard for you to obey the rules? What can you do that will help you be more obedient?

_____

_____

_____

_____

_____

_____

✛ ✛ ✛ ✛ ✛ ✛ ✛ ✛ ✛  ✛ ✛ ✛ ✛ ✛ ✛ ✛ ✛ ✛

What's the big deal about a few compromises?

Today's Teen: Samson
Today's Action Verse: Judges 14:9
Storyline: Judges 14:1–10

Samson Speaks Today: *"God doesn't see sins as little or big; sin is sin to Him. He even cares about what we think are 'little' sins. Little compromises lead to huge problems."*

✛ ✛ ✛ ✛ ✛ ✛ ✛ ✛ ✛ ✛ ✛ ✛ ✛ ✛ ✛ ✛ ✛ ✛ ✛ ✛

Digging Deeper: *What's the big deal about a little honey?* The problem wasn't that Samson ate honey; it was that he disregarded the commitment to God that comes with being a Nazirite. As a Nazirite, he was not to touch a dead body, but he had taken honey from the carcass of a lion! The issue was more significant than simply eating a little honey—the act was a blatant sin against God. I believe Samson knew what he was doing. This was just one of many steps Samson took that led him away from God.

Perhaps today you're thinking, *What's the big deal about _____?* Maybe it's a few drinks at a party, or a couple of smokes with friends at school, or watching a movie with sex and violence. You know it's wrong, but everyone else seems to think it's OK. You don't want to be different; you want to fit in. But, as Samson learned, a small violation of your values is a *big* step toward the miserable life, a big step toward a downward spiral of sin that hurts you and others you love too.

Just Like You: Joe, Sam, and Barry were talking about girls one day. The conversation went like this:

Joe: Do you think it's OK to give your girlfriend a good-night kiss?

Sam: I don't know. Doesn't seem so bad. Is there anywhere in the Bible that says you can't?

Joe: No, you just have to be careful not to get caught.

Sam: Yeah, you kind of have to be smart about it. I'd be careful.

Barry: (*Having soaked in this conversation, pipes up.*) I think you're looking at it all wrong.

Joe: What do you mean?

Barry: Well, I don't mean to act "holier than thou," but maybe the question shouldn't be, "What can we get away with?"

Sam: Well, shouldn't we figure out what we should and shouldn't do with a girl?

Barry: I just think we run into trouble when we try to get all around the edges of what we know we're not supposed to do.

Joe: So you think a good-night kiss is a big deal. I mean it's not like we're...

Barry: It's not the kiss, Joe. But when you start with that, you'll want to do more, and then soon, you're going down a path you really never wanted to travel.

Sam: I hear what you're saying, Barry. To guard our purity, we really shouldn't play around with those temptations.

Did You Know? Not all of Samson's great feats are recorded in the Book of Judges, but these were: killing the lion bare-handed (Judges 14:5–6); slaying 30 Philistines (14:19); catching 300 foxes and tying torches to their tails (15:3–5); breaking bonds (15:14; 16:9, 12, 14); slaying 1,000 men with the jawbone of a donkey (15:15); carrying off the Gaza city gate (16:3); and destroying the Philistine building (16:30). Judges 16:24 leads me to believe Samson did a lot more incredible things that weren't recorded.

Today's Prayer: *Dear Lord, I realize that all compromises and all sins are equally wrong and an affront to Your holiness and righteousness. Help me to be on guard against compromises that may undermine my walk with You.*

Journal Question: What compromises have you made recently? Was the payoff worth it? What reasons did you use to justify them?

DAY 38

Am I guarding the gateway to my soul?

Today's Teen: Samson
Today's Action Verses: Judges 14:1–2; 1 Thessalonians 4:3–5
Storyline: Judges 14

Samson Speaks Today: *"Guard what you allow before your eyes, and ask God for help in bringing your powerful lusts under the control of the Holy Spirit."*

Digging Deeper: When you read Samson's tragic story, it's obvious that Samson made some very destructive choices in his relationships with women. But Samson's problem wasn't sex; it was lust. Author and pastor, Joshua Harris, in his book *Not Even a Hint,* says this about the unquenchable thirst of lust: "Lust is always an unholy desire for the forbidden. But though lust longs for an object or a person, ultimately the object is not its prize; its goal is the very act of desiring. The result is that lust can never be quenched. As soon as the object of lust is attained, lust wants something more."

Samson failed to arm himself against the ravages of out-of-control lust in a world full of enticing temptations. He failed to guard his eyes and, in failing to do so, allowed lust to conquer his soul and give a foothold to the very enemy who sought his destruction.

You don't have to make this same mistake. You can begin by guarding your eyes. David said, *"I will set no wicked thing before mine eyes: I hate the work of them that turn aside; it shall not cleave to me"* (Psalms 101:3). David, too, experienced tragedy by not guarding his eyes, and he repented of that.

Just Like You: So you know you're supposed to guard your eyes, but that seems impossible, given the world of TV, movies, magazines, and the Internet that makes staying completely free of sexual images extremely challenging.

A few helpful pointers are listed here, but this list is not a legalistic set of do's and don'ts. It is a helpful guideline, but it will be useless if you don't rely upon the power of God to keep your heart and mind from temptation.

- Cancel subscriptions to teen magazines that constantly discuss sex outside of marriage and feature suggestive images and content.
- Ask your parents to help keep you accountable with your Internet usage. Use the Internet when other persons are around. Avoid anything-goes social networking sites.
- Ask your parents to install a good filter for your computer, and ask them to routinely monitor your Web traffic.
- Avoid television dramas or sitcoms that dwell on sex, even if it makes you seem out of the mainstream.
- Even when you're watching something harmless like a news show, documentary, or ball game, change the channel or turn the TV off if a commercial or other content is inappropriate.

Did You Know? Author Randy Alcorn shares these wise thoughts: "When it comes to causes of sin, don't just taper off, cut them off.... Don't be casual or gradual, be decisive. If that means never watching television, never going onto the Internet, never walking by a magazine rack, never going into a video store, never being with a certain person, or whatever, then make that resolution, no matter how radical or extreme it seems.... If these things seem like crutches, fine—use whatever crutches you need to help you walk."

Today's Prayer: *God, please help me guard my eyes, for I know they are the gateway to my heart.*

Journal Question: How can you guard the gateway to your soul today?

_____

_____

_____

_____

_____

_____

_____

Can God still use me if I've messed up my life?

Today's Teen: Samson
Today's Action Verses: Hebrews 11:32–34
Storyline: Judges 16:28–31

Samson Speaks Today: *"If you think you've really blown it—remember that your heavenly Father is a God of infinite mercy and grace. God will never leave or forsake you. He can always use you to do great things for Him."*

Digging Deeper: When you think of great Bible heroes, you might not think of Samson because of his tragic choices. But what does God think of Samson? Samson is listed as a hero in Hebrews 11, the chapter often called the Bible's Hall of Faith.

How can Samson be mentioned in the same breath as people like Moses, Deborah, and Gideon? The only reason is *grace*—that's one amazing word!

Grace is the radical concept that separates Christianity from other religions. Our God is a God of right and wrong and justice, but He's also a God of redemption and second chances. The very sins Samson committed were nailed to the cross by Jesus Christ.

At the end of his life, Samson asked God to do one more thing through him, a failed man. But in God's eyes, there is no such thing as damaged goods. If He can forgive Samson, He can forgive you—and use your life as an instrument for His glory.

The enemy wants you to sulk in your sin, wallow in your defeat, and mire in your mistakes. But God says you can have a fresh start. He loves you and really wants your life to be a success.

Just Like You: Elisabeth Elliot, in her best-selling classic, *Passion and Purity,* encourages those who've lost their purity and feel as though they are damaged goods, without hope of restoration in Christ:

> Have I nothing to say, then, to those who have already been in bed? I would have to have my head in the sand to imagine that my unmarried readers are all virgins. Those who have given away their virginity write to me, too, some of them in despair, feeling that they are forever banished from purity. I write to them to say that there is no purity in any of us apart from the blood of Jesus. All of us without exception are sinners and sinful, some in one way, some in another. If I can help some to avoid sin, I want to do that. If I can show others that the message of the Gospel is the possibility of a new birth and a new beginning and a new creation, I want to do that.
> —Elisabeth Elliot, *Passion and Purity* ✝

Did You Know? Samson defeated more enemies in his death than he did during all of his exploits in more than 20 years as a judge, showing that God sometimes accomplishes more out of our brokenness than out of our successes.

Today's Prayer: *Dear God, I know I've made many mistakes. I know I've sinned against You. I feel like I have shamed Your holy name. Please give me a second chance to shine for You.*

Journal Question: God promises you a fresh start today, but have you forgiven yourself? Use this space to write the things for which you need forgiveness—God's first, then your own. Now write words of praise to God for giving you a fresh new start.

_____

_____

_____

_____

_____

_____

_____

✠ ✢ ✠ ✠ ✠ ✠ ✠ ✠  ✠ ✢ ✠ ✠ ✠ ✠ ✠ ✠

DAY 40

How can I hear God's voice?

Today's Teen: Samuel
Today's Action Verse: 1 Samuel 3:10
Storyline: 1 Samuel 3

Samuel Speaks Today: *"If you tune your heart to God—He will speak to you, often in the quiet of the night."*

✠ ✢ ✠ ✠ ✠ ✠ ✠ ✢ ✠ ✠ ✠ ✠ ✠ ✠ ✠ ✠ ✠ ✠ ✠ ✠ ✢ ✢

Digging Deeper: God may not speak to you audibly like He did to Samuel, but you can be sure that God still pursues the hearts of young people, including yours, as relentlessly as He pursued Samuel's.

But something was different about Samuel. He wasn't like every other young person. His ears were ready to listen to God's voice. His heart was tuned to God's will. His feet were quick to follow the path God laid out for him.

God won't likely shout to get your attention. Sometimes He whispers gently in the night. Sometimes He speaks through a simple verse you come across in your daily devotions—a verse that slowly grips your heart and leads you down a path of spiritual understanding. He may speak through the encouraging words of a teacher in an otherwise boring class at school or through the lyrics of a song.

God is calling you to something bigger, better, and higher that He has prepared for you to do (Ephesians 2:8–10). He wants you, like Samuel, to make a difference in your generation. But to be a difference maker, your spirit needs to be tuned to God's frequency.

Just Like You: God might not speak to you audibly, in visions, in dreams, or by handwriting on the wall; however, God is still in the business of speaking to His people. He commonly uses other methods. Here are some ways God speaks to Christians today:

- **God speaks through His Word.** God spoke to Samuel and other Bible characters audibly because they didn't have the entire written Word of God. God's Word lays out most of what He wants you to do in life; God's Word provides pretty straightforward guidelines on living life.

- **God speaks through prayer.** If you're not talking to God, you won't hear Him talking to you. God speaks in the stillness, in the quiet, in the deep thoughtfulness of prayer. That's why it's so important to turn off the TV, crank down the iPod, put down the game controller, and spend time listening to the Lord.

- **God speaks through circumstances.** God is in control of everything that happens to you, without exception. That means God actually works out His will for your life through good and bad events—opportunities that arise, trials you face, and people you meet. These are all small pieces of the giant puzzle of your life.

- **God speaks through authority.** God uses your teachers, coaches, and, yes, parents to share His will for your life. Even if they make mistakes, even if they aren't perfect, and even if they aren't believers, God can use them. That's why obedience plays such an important role in order for you to hear God's voice.

Did You Know? God had not spoken to Israel in many years, mainly because of the terrible spiritual decay among Israel's leaders. But finally God found someone He could use—Samuel. Through Samuel, He again began a dialogue with His people.

Today's Prayer: *Dear God, I want to hear Your voice and know Your will. Draw me into Your presence.*

Journal Question: Have you listened to God's voice today? What is He saying to you?

_____

_____

_____

_____

_____

_____

_____

_____

_____

_____

_____

_____

_____

_____

_____

_____

_____

_____

DAY 41

How can I have my own relationship with God?

Today's Teen: Samuel
Today's Action Verse: 1 Samuel 2:18
Storyline: 1 Samuel 1:19; 3:1–10

Samuel Speaks Today: *"Growing up in a Christian home doesn't guarantee that you'll automatically serve God. You still have to choose to love God—on your own."*

✛ ✛ ✛ ✛ ✛ ✛ ✛ ✛ ✛ ✛ ✛ ✛ ✛ ✛ ✛ ✛ ✛ ✛ ✛ ✛

Digging Deeper: Even though Samuel had a godly mother and was mentored by a spiritual leader, Eli, his faith in God was not automatic. God's calling to Samuel in the middle of the night points out that faith in God is not just a tradition that gets passed down from family to family. Persons in each generation have to choose for themselves to walk with God.

Samuel was like many who grow up in church. People expect Christian young people to serve God naturally, as if the church were a factory that regularly churned out perfect people. But a relationship with God is not automatic. Christianity is not mechanical. Knowing God is a personal choice, an individual decision. Your parents can't do it for you. Your pastor can't do it for you. Your youth leader can't do it for you.

If you look at going to church and reading your Bible as things that you're *supposed* to do, you're missing out. God wants to have a relationship with you apart from your parents and apart from your church. He wants you.

You probably know by now that when you try to connect with God through your parents, pastor, or anyone else, you're not really experiencing true intimacy with God. You're living someone else's life, someone else's dreams, and someone else's gifts.

Just Like You: Chad grew up always knowing the difference between right and wrong. He went to a Christian school and his parents were active in a Bible-believing church. Chad remembers becoming a believer at the age of seven. He knew for sure he was going to heaven—but beyond that, his faith seemed more like a routine: Get up on Sunday morning and read a chapter or two from the Bible. Mutter a short prayer—the same one he muttered the day before. Put on his best clothes. Pile into the car with his four brothers, and go to church for a couple hours of preaching and teaching. He, from time to time, heard his parents and some friends talk about "walking with Jesus" or "knowing Jesus" or Jesus being their "best friend." But to him, it wasn't real. He believed in Jesus, but he didn't feel the personal experience others felt.

Am I doing this because I have to? What's the point? Chad often wondered, but never said aloud. One day, Chad finally worked up the courage to share his thoughts with his youth pastor. He was a bit embarrassed because he was supposed to be one of the "good kids."

Surprisingly, the youth pastor told him that he had struggled with the very same issues. Then the pastor pointed Chad to Psalm 13, in which David asked God, *"How long wilt thou forget me, O Lord? for ever? How long wilt thou hide thy face from me?"* (v. 1).

The key to knowing God personally, the youth pastor told Chad, is in talking directly to Him and telling Him your greatest fears, worries, and desires.

Did You Know? The name *Samuel* means "asked of God" or "heard of God." This shows us how serious Hannah, Samuel's mother, was about dedicating young Samuel to the Lord's work.

Today's Prayer: *Dear God, I want to walk with You and know You for myself. I know You care about my deepest needs and my deepest desires. I know You have a unique plan for me to prosper and grow.*

Journal Question: Does it seem like you do everything because your parents make you do it? How can you have a relationship with God that is truly personal?

_____

_____

_____

_____

_____

_____

Can God use Christian teens?

Today's Teen: Samuel
Today's Action Verses: 1 Samuel 2:35; 3:19–20
Storyline: 1 Samuel 3

Samuel Speaks Today: _"God is calling you to be a light in a dark world. Don't be afraid of the darkness—use it as an opportunity to shine the light of God's love to a hurting world."_

Digging Deeper: When God called Samuel, Israel was in spiritual decay (Judges 21:25). The men who were supposed to be spiritual leaders were failing. The temple had turned from a place of worship to a place of lewd entertainment. Eli, the priest, didn't stand firmly against the wickedness. His own sons proudly engaged in the sinful acts (1 Samuel 2:22; 3:13).

Israel was badly in need of young, fresh, godly leadership. Like Joseph and, later, David, Daniel, and Jeremiah, Samuel was called to rise up and be a spiritual giant in a heathen culture. Instead of succumbing to the temptations around him, Samuel was to stand tall and speak for God.

Sound familiar? Well, God is looking for the same leadership today. Modern society rejects God, embraces evil, and claims that there is no such thing as absolute truth. The world needs young men and women who are willing to stand for what they believe, in spite of criticism from peers, ungodly media, and the worldly culture.

Can you be this person? Can you be a Samuel? Can God use you to have an impact for Christ in your school, home, and community?

Just Like You: Twin teens Alex and Brett Harris are outspoken Christians who have started a movement called The Rebelution. On their Web site, therebelution.com, they encourage teens to grow up and be leaders. Here are some tips they offer on growing up:

- **Learn to manage your current responsibilities.** Do you let stress in one area of life spill over into your interaction with younger siblings and family members? If you can't keep your sense of humor and interest in others during the stresses of homework, don't expect to be able to when the stresses of college, marriage, career, and family weigh on your shoulders. He who would be faithful in much, must first prove himself faithful in little. Learn and practice good time management skills to allow time for the truly important things. Cut back on activities and pastimes that isolate you and absorb large amounts of time but accomplish little. Things like TV, surfing the web, reading magazines, watching movies, etc.... Remember that God does not give us conflicting responsibilities.
- **Choose your companions wisely.** Spend time with the type of grown ups you would like to become. Surround yourselves with friends who understand the importance of learning responsibility at an early age and encourage one another in your pursuit of maturity. Remember that your companions are not limited to people.
- **Pursue progressively greater responsibilities.** In a society where responsibility is not expected, young people are rarely given the opportunity to develop the maturity necessary to

become a responsible adult. Discipline yourself to pursue and accept progressively greater responsibility. This is the way we grow.

Growing up spoils childhood, only if childhood is misunderstood. If childhood is about having everything you could possibly want, with no responsibility, the result is adultescents, who avoid "growing up" at all costs. But if childhood is about preparation, as it has historically been defined, the result is great men and women who define adulthood as it should be defined: As the *fulfillment* of childhood. With such an understanding, growing up is not to be avoided, but pursued.

—Alex and Brett Harris, The Rebelution 1 Timothy 4:12 Web site ⊹

Did You Know? Eli was a descendant of Aaron, Moses's brother, through Aaron's fourth son, Ithamar. Eli and his sons were called as Levites to uphold their duties in the temple. But Eli's sons abused their spiritual authority, and their father did not properly discipline them.

Today's Prayer: *Dear God, help me to be active, mature, and influential during my teen years. Help me to rise up and be a leader in the world to which You have called me.*

Journal Question: How can you be a Samuel today?

_____

_____

_____

_____

_____

_____

_____

_____

DAY 43

Why do I have to listen to authority?

Today's Teen: Samuel
Today's Action Verse: 1 Samuel 3:1
Storyline: 1 Samuel 3

Samuel Speaks Today: *"If you listen to your spiritual leaders, you'll be listening to God, because God speaks through the men and women He chooses to put over you."*

Digging Deeper: Because Samuel was obedient to Eli, the priest, and because Samuel listened to the voice of God, God called Samuel for a very special purpose. It was not a coincidence that Samuel first thought Eli was calling him. *He was accustomed to listening to the voice of his spiritual leader.* This was how God brought Samuel to the next step in his life. By faithful obedience, listening to wise counsel, and applying truths to his personal life, Samuel had prepared himself for God's calling.

It's easy to disregard your parents, pastor, or teachers, considering them old-fashioned and out of touch. So why listen to anyone? It makes much more sense to do things your own way. But God has placed these people in your life for your own good. These wise, spiritual mentors have wisdom gained from lifetimes of walking with God. Proverbs 1:8–9 says their guidance is like a treasure: *"My son, hear the instruction of thy father, and forsake not the law of thy mother: for they shall be an ornament of grace unto thy head, and chains about thy neck."*

Samuel was blessed by following Eli as Eli directed Samuel to God, and you, too, will be blessed by following spiritual leaders who direct you to God. There are no shortcuts—no alternative routes to success.

Just Like You: In Romans 13:1–2, we discover that every authority is God given, even if every authority is not necessarily godly or even Christian. Here are some helpful pointers from the Bible that show you why obedience is really the only path to success:

- Every level of authority was divinely put in place by God—so to rebel against authority is to rebel against God (Romans 13:1–2).
- A lack of authority is not real freedom. Truth is the way to real freedom (John 8:32).
- Submitting to God-given authority helps you establish respect and credibility in the eyes of men (1 Peter 2:13–17).
- Submitting to godly authority is wise and fruitful (James 3:17).
- Obeying God helps you resist the devil (James 4:7). If you're obeying God, you're on the winning side. If you're disobeying God, you're embracing the devil and siding with him against God—not the best side to be on!

Your attitude toward authority reveals your attitude toward God. You cannot be in open rebellion against God-appointed authority and be in fellowship with God.

The Seven Checkpoints for Youth Leaders, by Andy Stanley and Stuart Hall, offers some valuable tips to help you obey authority. Here are a few ideas gathered from that book:

- Remember that it's not what you're being asked to do, but who is doing the asking.
- Write down a list of authority figures you seem to clash with.
- Ask yourself these questions:
  Do they ask you to do things that are wrong?
  Do they ask you to do things beyond your abilities?
  Are their requests unreasonable?
  Is your problem with them, or is it that you don't like being told what to do?

Did You Know? Samuel had the distinction of being a prophet, a priest, and a judge.

Today's Prayer: *God, give me the courage to obey authority. I know that each level of authority in my life has been allowed by You to guide me along Your perfect will.*

Journal Question: What authority figures do you seem to clash with? What do you need to change about your attitude toward authority?

_____

_____

_____

_____

✛ ✛ ✛ ✛ ✛ ✛ ✛ ✛ ✛   ✛ ✛ ✛ ✛ ✛ ✛ ✛ ✛ ✛

Can God use someone from a broken home?

Today's Teen: Samuel
Today's Action Verses: 1 Samuel 1:1–2
Storyline: 1 Samuel 1:1–17

Samuel Speaks Today: *"It really doesn't matter what your home life looks like, because God can take you from any situation and raise you up to be a person of influence in this generation."*

✛ ✛

Digging Deeper: If you think your family life is rough, consider Samuel's. His father had two wives. His stepmom routinely feuded with his mom.

And his surrogate father, Eli, had sons whom he couldn't control; they were always getting into trouble.

The bottom line is that God often calls young people out of broken homes and broken families. If you think you have to have a perfect family life to accomplish anything great, then you haven't read about too many of God's great heroes, such as Joseph, Samuel, Josiah, Ruth, Esther, and others. Each of them followed God, in spite of family difficulties. Fortunately, Samuel had a godly mother whose prayer and devotion must have lit his fire of faith.

If you have a heart for God, He'll use your life, no matter where you've come from. God provided Samuel with a godly mother and with Eli as a mentor. God can do the same for you. Perhaps your parents are divorced. Or maybe they have other problems. Maybe they don't go to church. Even so, God can bring people into your life who can help you grow into the young woman or young man He wants you to be.

If you do have a godly mother and father, don't take this blessing for granted. Treasure them.

Just Like You: Shaunti feels a little out of place in her Christian school. It seems that all her friends come from perfect, intact Christian homes, unlike hers. Her family life seems so dysfunctional. Her dad walked out on them when she was three, leaving her mom to raise three children. Her brother can't seem to stay out of trouble... or jail. Her younger sister is pregnant. At school, she hears the constant drumbeat of gossip and whispers about her family's latest bad news. Sometimes, she doesn't even want to go to school. She'd rather crawl in a hole somewhere and hide.

Shaunti really wants to do something great for God, but she feels trapped in a messy family. *Can God use me?* she wonders. *Would He even want me? My dad isn't a big-shot pastor or spiritual leader. My mother is struggling just to keep her faith. My siblings are always in trouble.*

Shaunti and countless teens like her can take comfort in God's love. God doesn't pull all His servants from "ideal" or "perfect" families. In fact, God often gets His greatest leaders from obscure, broken, messy homes. Just ask Samuel.

Did You Know? Elkanah, Samuel's father, took a second wife, Peninnah, apparently because Hannah could not bear children. Inability to bear children was considered a curse, and it was customary for the husband of a barren wife to take a second wife. Polygamy (the practice of having two or more mates) was common back then. However, God's ideal plan is marriage between one man and one woman (Genesis 2:18–24).

Today's Prayer: *Dear God, I know You love me. Thank You for planning my life before the world began. I know You can use me, no matter what the state of my family is.*

Journal Question: What are some ways God can turn a dysfunctional family experience into something to encourage others?

_____

_____

_____

_____

_____

_____

_____

_____

_____

_____

_____

_____

_____

_____

_____

_____

_____

_____

Can I be a leader as a teen?

Today's Teen: Samuel
Today's Action Verses: 1 Samuel 3:19; 1 Timothy 4:12
Storyline: 1 Samuel 3

Samuel Speaks Today: *"It's never too early to stand up and be a spiritual leader."*

Digging Deeper: Samuel was only a child when God called him to be the spiritual leader of Israel. Like David, Solomon, Jeremiah, Josiah, Timothy, and Esther, God equipped Samuel with maturity and wisdom beyond his years to be a spiritual leader in a dark world. These examples show you don't have to have gray hair and an aching back to do something for Christ.

Would you like more examples of youth in leadership roles? Charles Spurgeon was 17 when he preached his first sermon, 18 when he took his first church, and 20 when he became pastor of the New Park Street Chapel in London. David Farragut, the US Navy's first admiral, became a midshipman on the warship Essex by the age of 10; at the age of 12, he was given command of his first ship. The father of our country, George Washington, was named official surveyor for Culpepper County, Virginia, at the age of 16. Phillis Wheatley, though brought to America as a slave child, was the first African American to publish a book. She published her first poem at age 12. Mary "Molly Pitcher" Hays, was a teen bride who later joined her husband on the battlefield at Valley Forge, and carried water to the weary troops of George Washington's army.

The aging Apostle Paul offered these words of encouragement to a frightened young preacher named Timothy: *"Let no man despise thy youth; but be thou an example of the believers, in word, in conversation, in charity, in spirit, in faith, in purity"* (1 Timothy 4:12).

Just Like You: In October 2005, Noah Riner, president of the Dartmouth College student body, stood before the class of incoming freshmen and began sharing what many thought would be the traditional speech. He lauded the class of 2009 as being smart, talented, and special. But then, his speech veered off from the usually schmaltzy, feel-good lectures that freshmen usually hear: "It isn't enough to be special. It isn't enough to be talented, to be beautiful, to be smart." Riner said none of these traits matters, without character. Then Riner continued with what became a very controversial section of his speech: "Character has a lot to do with sacrifice, laying our personal interests down for something bigger. The best example of this is Jesus. In the Garden of Gethsemane, just hours before His crucifixion, Jesus prayed, *'Father, if thou be willing, remove this cup from me: nevertheless not my will, but thine, be done.'* He knew the right thing to do. He knew the cost would be agonizing torture and death. He did it anyway. That's character. Jesus is a good example of character, but He's also much more than that. He is the Solution to flawed people."

Soon, Noah became the subject of intense ridicule from newspapers, political pundits, bloggers, and many of the students at Dartmouth. One student body officer resigned in protest. The universal question on everyone's mind was this: *How could Noah Riner stand up there and talk about Jesus?*

Noah also received many encouraging emails from fellow Christian students not only at Dartmouth but around the world. They thanked him for standing up for truth and sharing Christ. Noah Riner didn't allow his youth to stand in the way of his commitment to Christ.

Did You Know? Samuel was raised by his mother until he was three; then he was taken to the temple to be groomed for the priesthood. This fulfilled a promise that Hannah made to God before Samuel was born.

Today's Prayer: *Dear God, help me to be a leader in my school, my home, my church, and my community. Please don't let me use my youth as an excuse to put off the important work of serving You.*

Journal Question: How can you be a leader in school, at home, or at church?

_____

_____

_____

_____

_____

_____

_____

_____

DAY
46

✠ ✝ ✠ ✚ ✠ ✠ ✠ ✠ ✠ ✠   ✠ ✝ ✠ ✠ ✠ ✠ ✠ ✠ ✠

Does it matter how I treat older people?

Today's Teen: Samuel
Today's Action Verse: 1 Samuel 3:15
Storyline: 1 Samuel 3:11–18

Samuel Speaks Today: *"You might not understand older people, but don't disrespect them. You'll be surprised how much they know and how much wisdom they can give you about the journeys you will take in life."*

✠ ✝ ✠ ✠ ✠ ✠ ✠ ✠ ✠ ✠ ✠ ✠ ✠ ✠ ✠ ✝ ✠ ✠ ✠ ✠ ✠ ✠ ✝

Digging Deeper: After his encounter with God, Samuel should have been glad, but the message he received from the Lord that night weighed heavily upon the young guy's heart. The message he received carried grave news for Eli, Samuel's mentor, spiritual leader, and surrogate father. How could he possibly tell Eli?

Young Samuel, called by God, chosen as Israel's next spiritual leader, gifted for great work, had profound respect for his elders. He had a reverence for Eli that surpassed that of Eli's own sons, who shamed their father by openly sinning in the house of the Lord. What separated Samuel from his peers was that he knew his place in the world. I think his actions show not only that he understood that older people are a treasure, not a nuisance, but also that reverencing the previous generation brings greater wisdom and a longer life.

What is your attitude toward the older people in your life? Society preaches rebellion and open mockery of the traditional ways of your parents. But God says that respect for your elders is healthy, wise, and beneficial.

Just Like You: Frank really wanted to earn money in the summer between his junior and senior years of high school, but the availability of jobs for guys was quickly evaporating. It seemed like the stores had all their summer help, the fast-food restaurants weren't hiring, and his small town did not provide many office jobs. But one day, Frank's dad came home with good news. Frank's dad was a realtor who owned his own business. He had just hired an 80-year-old realtor, named Ernest, who couldn't drive, but needed to get around from house to house. If Frank was willing to be Ernest's driver, Frank could not only make some money, but he'd probably also get in all the required driving hours for his license.

At first, Frank thought the job would be pretty lame. But after a few days on the job, Frank found Ernest to be quite engaging. Plus, Ernest didn't wag his finger and look down on young people. In fact, he was a lot of fun. Not only did he share tales about his military service in World War II, he also offered to help Frank with history—a subject Frank seemed to struggle with. Frank was surprised at how much fun an 80-year-old guy could actually be.

When the summer was over and Frank had to go back to school, he sent his dad an email: "Dad, I just want to thank you for the opportunity to drive Ernest around this summer. At first, I thought it would be a complete bore, but Ernest and I are actually pretty good friends. He taught me a lot of stuff about life."

Did You Know? With God's revelation to Samuel, God was no longer speaking to Israel through Eli, the priest. Because of his son's failures, Eli could no longer be the spiritual leader in Israel. God was, as of that time, raising up Samuel.

Today's Prayer: *Dear God, I don't always understand the ways of older people, but help me to respect them and listen to their advice. I know someday I'll be glad I did.*

Journal Question: Who are some of the older and "out-of-touch" people who annoy you the most? What are some ways you can reach out to them and learn from their wisdom?

_____

_____

_____

_____

_____

_____

_____

_____

_____

_____

_____

_____

_____

✦ ✦ ✦ ✦ ✦ ✦ ✦ ✦ ✦ ✦   ✦ ✦ ✦ ✦ ✦ ✦ ✦ ✦ ✦ ✦

Does church matter anymore?

Today's Teen: Samuel
Today's Action Verse: 1 Samuel 2:26
Storyline: 1 Samuel 2:22–35

Samuel Speaks Today: *"Just because your church isn't perfect doesn't mean you should give up on it. **Be** the change you want to **see**."*

✦ ✦

Digging Deeper: Samuel grew up around a religious institution that had drifted far from God's original plan. Eli allowed his sons to pervert the temple with their partying and immorality.

To put Samuel's religious experience in modern English, the church had failed him. He had every reason to chuck his faith and abandon God. There was no reality, no authenticity—just a bunch of people in a giant faith charade.

Sound familiar? Churches seem to include some people who say one thing on Sunday and do another thing on Monday. Maybe this is your experience. Has the church failed you? Maybe you've been hurt by binding legalism. Maybe you've been hurt by a trusted spiritual leader. Or it could be that you've never seen the reality of Christ lived out in anyone.

Like Samuel, you have every reason to give up on the faith. But before you quit, take a long look at Samuel. Even in the haze of phoniness surrounding him, he was able to discover that God is real.

Maybe God wants you to be a difference maker too. Instead of running from the church, maybe you can stand up and change the church culture by showing how real God is in your life.

Just Like You: A lot of Christians are wondering about the validity of church these days: *Does church still matter in the twenty-first century? Can't we just listen to a few messages on the Internet or read the Bible at home?* That sounds good, but that philosophy has some serious flaws. Church still matters for several reasons:

- **First of all, the church is not the building, it's the people.** God created you and me to serve Him in *community,* not *isolation.* Living out your faith in community means giving to others and receiving from them. That is done through the local church.
- **For all of its warts and problems, the local church is** *still* **where God chooses to work in this age.** The church is His divine institution, the body of Christ.
- **Changing times should draw you** *to* **the church rather than pull you** *away from* **the church.** Why? Because the church, even with all its imperfections, is a lighthouse, a beacon, an anchor in a stormy world.
- **The church is where you can find the wisest, godliest spiritual leadership.** The wisdom of men and women of God can and will help you find and discern God's will.
- **The church is a team.** People can effect more change in the world when they work together.

Did You Know? The word that the original Scripture used for *sin* when referring to Eli's sons implies that they weren't ignorantly sinning, but were willfully sinning against God openly in the temple.

Today's Prayer: *Dear God, help me to look beyond the hypocrisy and phoniness of others and see You for who You really are.*

Journal Question: Why does church even matter? What are some ways church matters to you specifically?

_____

_____

_____

_____

_____

DAY 48

Do my friends really have an influence on my life?

Today's Teen: Samuel
Today's Action Verse: 1 Samuel 2:26
Storyline: 1 Samuel 2

Samuel Speaks Today: *"Your friends are who you are. Choose them wisely so you will follow the wisest and most successful path."*

Digging Deeper: Imagine how hard it was for Samuel to live out his faith. Sure, he grew up in the temple, but the temple was defiled with all kinds of sinful activities and bizarre pagan practices. And it doesn't seem that there were any good friends around to hang with. Eli's sons were ringleaders of the party-all-the-time atmosphere.

Apparently Samuel, as best he could, chose to avoid influences that would bring him down. He could have hung out with Eli's sons, but he didn't. This means Samuel probably had few friends.

Sometimes teens have to make this tough choice. You want to have good friends, but what if there really are no spiritual guys or girls in your school? Samuel hung out with Eli, even though Eli was many years older than he was.

If you choose to hang out only with people who share your values, you may have to be alone often or get comfortable being with people who are older. That doesn't mean you shouldn't be friendly with persons who don't know the Lord. That doesn't mean you should think you're better than everyone else. But you must not allow the wrong values of others to influence your values.

Just Like You: When should you *stop* hanging out with a friend? You want to be a good friend and be there through thick and thin. But what do you do when your best friend is making choices that are just plain wrong? How do you stop him or her from being a bad influence on you? Walking the tightrope between judging others and having wisdom can be difficult and dangerous, so here are a few pointers:

- **Make sure you're not being overly critical.** If the issue of concern is just an annoying habit, that's no reason to stop being someone's friend. After all, you have annoying quirks too!
- **Be honest and real by talking face-to-face with your friend.** Confront the person about the bad choices he or she is making. If you use a polite but firm approach, he or she may reconsider those bad actions, especially if that person knows continuing the actions could cost your friendship.
- **Help when the friend wants help.** If your friend is struggling but asking for help, this is the time to be an even greater friend, by taking your friend's problems to a parent or a spiritual leader.
- **Note your friend's attitude.** If your friend has a carefree attitude about breaking the rules and makes fun of you for wanting to do right, then you know it's time to part ways. Remember, that person is not being a true friend, because he or she is choosing lifestyle over your friendship.
- **Don't make a public spectacle of the issue.** It is sometimes easy and tempting to tell a bunch of people about your friend's wrongdoing and make yourself out to be a hero, but doing that is just as wrong as the choices your friend is making.
- **Pray for your friend.** Ask God to work in your friend's heart to help him or her see the need to repent and come back to the Lord.

Did You Know? Samuel was one of the examples in the Bible that shows us that God has a plan for us before our birth. Samuel was called before birth for special service. Other examples are Jacob, Samson, Jeremiah, and John the Baptist.

Today's Prayer: *Dear Lord, help me to make wise decisions regarding my friends and to stop hanging around bad influences. Give me courage and humility with those friends I may have to cut off. Thank you for the plans you have for me.*

Journal Question: Why was it so hard for Samuel to live out his faith? Are you willing to give up friends if that's what it takes to live for God?

_____

_____

_____

_____

✛ ✛ ✛ ✛ ✛ ✛ ✛ ✛ ✛ ✛ ✛ ✛ ✛ ✛ ✛ ✛ ✛

Am I willing to do the hard things in life to succeed?

Today's Teen: Samuel
Today's Action Verse: 1 Samuel 3:18
Storyline: 1 Samuel 3:15–18

Samuel Speaks Today: *"If you want what's best for those you love, sometimes you have to tell them what they may not want to hear."*

✛ ✛ ✛ ✛ ✛ ✛ ✛ ✛ ✛ ✛ ✛ ✛ ✛ ✛ ✛ ✛ ✛ ✛ ✛ ✛

Digging Deeper: The message God gave young Samuel wasn't a pleasant one. He had to go tell Eli, his mentor and second father, that God was going to judge Eli's house for the behavior of his sons. Eventually the entire family line would be killed. This was not the type of prophecy Samuel was looking forward to sharing.

But Samuel was faithful to God and, with a heavy heart and humble spirit, shared God's message with Eli. Do you think he might have been very nervous? I can imagine him practicing his speech. Could he have doubted himself and wished he could make it all go away? The main thing to see in this account is that Samuel did what he had to do in the most humble and loving way.

Has God given you a tough job like Samuel's? Is a friend or relative doing something wrong and you need to help him or her get back on the right track? Maybe you're afraid you'll jeopardize the relationship. Better that relationship than your relationship with God.

Walking with God and being a good friend sometimes mean doing hard things—things you'd rather pawn off on someone else. But this is what it takes to be a leader.

Just Like You: Alex and Brett Harris, on their Rebelution blog (therebelution. com), say this about doing hard things:

> We've all been asked the question, "Are you willing to lose your life for Christ?" Perhaps we've heard it from our youth pastor, our parents, asked ourselves while reading *Voice of the Martyrs,* or read or watched a Christian book or movie which revolves around the question.
>
> As emotionally invasive and as spiritually relevant as that question is, I often find myself thinking that *dying* for Christ isn't the question. Instead, my challenge to us is: "Are we willing to live for Christ?" This is not unconnected from the question of dying for Christ, but is the first question we must ask ourselves.
>
> Whether I am able to bench 200 lbs. is a good question. But first I must be able to honestly say I can bench 100 lbs. Whether I am able to run a marathon is a good question. But first I must be able to honestly say I can run a mile.
>
> Let me put it another way: I cannot trust God when my two-month-old niece passes away if I am not trusting Him when I stub my toe. I will not be able to trust God in the big storms if I have been trying to stand on my own through the small ones.

We must all be willing to die for Christ. But before that is possible we must be able to say with the Apostle Paul, "For to me to **live** is Christ, [**therefore**] to **die** is gain."

Living for Christ is the prerequisite of dying for Christ. Obedience when no one is watching comes before obedience in public. And I'm talking about obedience that's hard—obedience that costs you something. That is why you can't fake hard things, and that is why small hard things always come before big hard things.

—Alex and Brett Harris, The Rebelution 1 Timothy 4:12 Web site

Did You Know? Samuel repeated Eli's parenting mistakes and raised sons who turned their backs on God. This was one of the many factors that led Israel to reject God's direct system of government and demand a king.

Today's Prayer: *Dear God, please give me the courage to do the hard things in life.*

Journal Question: What are some hard things God may be calling you to do?

_____

_____

_____

_____

_____

_____

_____

_____

_____

_____

_____

_____

_____

Do I have to be popular for God to use me?

Today's Teen: David
Today's Action Verse: Psalm 78:7
Storyline: 1 Samuel 16:1–3

David Speaks Today: *"It doesn't matter who you are or where you have come from: God sees you and has an incredible plan for your life."*

Digging Deeper: God's choice for David to be Israel's next king probably made people scratch their heads. Of all the persons in the world, David was the last guy anyone would have picked. He was just a young, ruddy shepherd boy.

Even Samuel, though a godly man, didn't see much in David. But God wasn't only choosing the next ruler; He was choosing a ruler whom He would work through to establish a legacy of godliness and faithfulness for the rest of Israel's history. Out of this king's family would come the Messiah. We know that Messiah to be Jesus.

This next king had to have a heart for God. That's why David was such an easy choice. He may not have been as flashy as his brothers. He may not have been a strong soldier. All we know that he could do at the time he was chosen was play music and lead sheep. But David had something his brothers didn't. He knew God in a very personal way. And even then, he was not perfect. He failed. But he loved God.

A heart for God can take you anywhere God wants you to go, even if you're not the most popular person in your school, church, or neighborhood.

Why? Because God sees the real you. He knows you. And He wants to do things with your life you never dreamed were possible.

Just Like You: Kate just knew that this school year would be awful. Her parents were going through a divorce. She was forced to move away from the school and friends she knew and loved. She was having to start her senior year trying to fit in wherever she could. Kind of shy, she worried what the other students would say. Would they laugh at her? Would anyone be her friend? Would they think she was weird because she went to church?

The night before her first day at school, Kate was miserable. Clothes were scattered around her room as she tried to find an outfit that would make her look good. But every time she stepped in front of the mirror with a different outfit on, she burst into tears, thinking, *I'm ugly, and they'll all laugh at me.*

The next morning, Kate woke up and found a piece of paper under her door. It was a note from her mom. She picked it up and read, "Kate, I know you don't have much confidence today, so I wanted you to take this verse with you to school. *'I will praise thee; for I am fearfully and wonderfully made'* (Psalm 139:14). Thousands of years ago, a young teen named David had the same doubts and fears that you have. Please know that I'm praying for you."

Did You Know? David was anointed king with special anointing oil. It represented holiness and was used to mark kings, judges, and priests as being set apart for God's service.

Today's Prayer: *Lord, I know You accept me just the way I am. Help me to work on what is most important: my heart.*

Journal Question: What really makes someone popular or favored in the eyes of men? What about in the eyes of God?

_____

_____

_____

_____

_____

_____

DAY 51

Why does God wait so long to fulfill His promises?

Today's Teen: David
Today's Action Verse: 1 Samuel 16:13
Storyline: 2 Samuel 5

David Speaks Today: *"If God makes a promise, He'll keep it, even if it takes a while to come to pass."*

Digging Deeper: David was in his midteens, perhaps 16, when God chose him to be Israel's second king, but he didn't actually become king until he was 30. That's 14 years or longer! Assuming Samuel told David why he was being anointed, imagine how hard it must have been for David to focus on the day-to-day tasks of shepherding, serving, and battling while he waited for God's plan to unfold! Imagine how many nights David might have lain awake dreaming of the palace! Imagine the times David could have doubted God's plan! I imagine that David often wondered why God didn't make him king right away. God's ways don't always make sense to us.

Has God put an unfulfilled desire in your heart? Maybe He's shared His purpose for your life, but all the doors seem to be closing. When your dream seems to drift off and die, when you get tired of the day-to-day tasks of your ordinary life, when you're ready to give up on God, remember God is faithful. He fulfilled His purpose for David, and He'll do it for you.

Just Like You: Waiting was part of the plan for most of the teens in the Bible who were called by God for a special purpose. Consider Moses, Joseph, and David and their waiting times:

- God brought **Moses** to Pharaoh's house to help prepare him for His plan, which included leading the children of Israel from bondage. But Moses had to leave Egypt in a rush and wait a long 40 years before coming back to fulfill God's plan.
- As a young man, **Joseph** dreamt about God's special plan for him, but he had to wait 13 trying years before God made him the prime minister of Egypt, fulfilling his dreams.
- As a teen, **David** was anointed to be the next king of Israel, but he didn't sit on the throne until he was 30.

Here are some helpful ways to make your waiting time useful:
- **Improve your life by reading, studying, and learning** from the best leaders in the area into which God is leading you.
- **Take every opportunity to serve,** even in a menial capacity, to gain experience in the area God put on your heart.
- **Do the small things well,** proving you are faithful to God and to others by working hard.
- **Stay humble and teachable.**

Did You Know? The Bible says the Holy Spirit came upon David and departed from Saul. In the Old Testament, God selectively sent the Spirit upon individuals to accomplish a specific purpose. At the time of Pentecost in Acts 2, God sent the Holy Spirit down to all the believers, and now everyone who believes in Jesus as Savior is automatically indwelt with the Spirit (Ephesians 4:30).

Today's Prayer: *God, I know You have a plan, and I trust Your plan. Give me grace to endure while I'm waiting for it to transpire.*

Journal Question: Why do you think you have to wait for God to reveal His will to you? What can you do in the meantime?

_____

_____

_____

_____

_____

_____

_____

_____

✛ ✛ ✛ ✛ ✛ ✛ ✛ ✛ ✛   ✛ ✛ ✛ ✛ ✛ ✛ ✛ ✛

Are my teen years that important?

Today's Teen: David
Today's Action Verse: Colossians 3:23
Storyline: 1 Samuel 16:14–23

David Speaks Today: *"Don't sit around waiting for something to happen. Take every opportunity to improve yourself."*

✛ ✛ ✛ ✛ ✛ ✛ ✛ ✛ ✛ ✛ ✛ ✛ ✛ ✛ ✛ ✛ ✛ ✛ ✛ ✛

Digging Deeper: Specific criteria were considered when Saul's personal musician was being chosen: the candidate suggested, David, was a gifted musician, strong and valiant young man of war, wise, and good looking, and the Lord was with him.

How did David develop these qualities and characteristics? For one thing, he didn't just waste away his teen years seeking pleasure. He lived intentionally and became a champion for God.

Many people say you can wait until later in life to get serious. But this myth will rob you of the best years of your life and keep you from having your dreams fulfilled. You can be serious about God and still enjoy your youth.

Don't wait; choose today to live for God.

Just Like You: What are some wise choices you can make as a young person?

- **Read.** Each week, substitute an hour or two of television with an hour or two of reading. Reading stretches your mind and can give you wisdom beyond your years.
- **Talk with older persons.** Ask teachers, pastors, and business people questions about their jobs or issues in the news. You will benefit from their years of experience and insight.
- **Volunteer.** Look for opportunities to volunteer, whether at church or in the community. This will give you chances to meet new people and discover gifts and talents you never knew you had.
- **Develop your skills.** If you have particular skills or interests in music, art, writing, or mechanical stuff, set aside time to hone your skills by practicing, studying, and learning.

Did You Know? Because King Saul disobeyed God, God took the kingdom from him and gave it to David. David was a man after God's own heart, and God made plans for the future Messiah, Jesus, to be born from David's lineage, not from the family of the first king of Israel, Saul.

Today's Prayer: *Dear Lord, help me use my teen years to prepare well for life.*

Journal Question: Are you putting off until later any spiritual decisions that need to be made? What decisions are they? How can you start now to prepare for the rest of your life?

_____

_____

_____

_____

_____

_____

_____

_____

DAY 53

How can I connect with God?

Today's Teen: David
Today's Action Verse: Acts 13:22
Storyline: 1 Samuel 16:14–23

David Speaks Today: *"There is nothing as exciting and adventurous as a relationship with God."*

Digging Deeper: *"The Lord is with him."* These five words described David (1 Samuel 16:18). Everyone around David knew something special was going on inside this young man. His walk with God was real. It affected the way he lived. It was a part of who he was.

Have you ever met someone like this? Someone whose faith just oozes out for all to see? I'm not talking about someone who brags about how good he or she is or who is always telling everyone how to live. In fact, most people who are really close to God are sort of quiet about it, but their attitudes and service speak volumes about what is going on inside.

What is the *one thing* your friends say about you? Do they know that you love God? Is it evident in your life? Is it obvious, not just by bumper stickers, a fish symbol on your car, or the Christian T-shirts you wear, but by a real live relationship with the Creator of the universe?

Just Like You: Author and Bible teacher Elmer Towns, in his book *How to Pray,* has these encouraging words for those who want to begin a deeper connection with God:

> I often hear people say, "I can't pray." They just don't seem to know where to start or what they should say to God. Well, the point is

not to focus on what we can't do but on what we can do. If all we can say is "God," then we can start there. If we can recite Psalm 23, "The Lord is my shepherd," then we can start there. In fact, we don't even have to say anything. Just coming into God's presence is praying.

Some of us think that we have to get everything in our lives *just right* before we can pray. But that's not the way it is at all. Look at the story of the thief who was dying on the cross next to Jesus. The only thing that he knew about Jesus was that Christ was the Lord. So the thief just said, "Lord, remember me when You come into Your kingdom" (Luke 23:42 [NKJV]). It's not the formula of the words we utter that matters, but rather our willingness to open up our heart to God.

—Elmer L. Towns, *How to Pray* ⚬

Did You Know? The name *David* is a common name today, but it was unique among the Jewish people. You'll notice that Jesse's son, David, is the only David in the Bible. In the Hebrew it means "beloved."

Today's Prayer: *Dear God, I just want to come into Your presence. I want to connect with You in a way that allows others to see the evidence of Your hand upon my life.*

Journal Question: Why does connecting with God seem so hard? Why does God seem so distant and unreal? What can you do to develop a more personal relationship with Him?

_____

_____

_____

_____

_____

_____

_____

DAY 54

Does music have that much influence on my life?

Today's Teen: David
Today's Action Verse: Psalm 108:1
Storyline: 1 Samuel 16:14–23

David Speaks Today: *"Music is a powerful influence on your life, so choose music that brings you closer to God."*

Digging Deeper: Music wasn't just an important part of David's life; I dare say, music was David's life. He wrote some of the most-used, most-loved, most-quoted pieces of lyric and song ever written.

During those long days in the shepherd fields, music was David's outlet of expression. When David sang, he communicated to his heavenly Father all that was in his heart. And today when we read his psalms, they often voice what is in our hearts.

Music can draw us closer to God. But the enemy perverts music. Satan, knowing the power of music upon the human heart, has an alternate purpose. Instead of bringing us closer to our Creator, the music of the enemy drives our soul away from the Savior.

When you're unsure of what CD to buy or which songs to download, ask these important questions:

- Are the words spiritually uplifting?
- What actions does this music provoke?
- Does the music itself point me to the Savior and to good thoughts or to bad?

- Does the theme expressed in the song conflict with what I know about the Bible?

Just Like You: Carlos loves music. Hardly an hour goes by without him listening to one of his favorite Christian artists. Carlos downloads songs, plays the guitar, and enjoys singing with the praise team at church.

But Carlos is also very discerning about the music he downloads to his iPod. Why? Because he understands the value of good music and the destructive power of bad music.

Sometimes Carlos is forced to take an unpopular stand. When his friends want to tune in to a secular rap station, Carlos says no. When he's invited to a concert by a musical group whose values are in opposition to those in the Bible, Carlos says no. When he's given a questionable CD for a birthday gift, Carlos accepts it with thanks, but takes it back to the music store and exchanges it for a more acceptable one. It isn't that Carlos is trying to act better than everyone else; he's just very careful about what he allows into his heart, soul, and mind. Like David, he's very aware of the power of music.

Did You Know? The harp was a popular instrument in Israel, and David became famed for his ability to play it. But the instrument called a harp in the Bible was simpler than what is known as a harp today; it was more like a lyre and was portable. Such instruments had a sound chest as the base. A rod, curved or straight, arose from each end. These two rods were connected above by a crosspiece, and the strings were stretched upward from the base to the crosspiece.

Today's Prayer: *Dear Lord, please guide my musical choices. Help me to use music to praise You and draw my heart into Your presence.*

Journal Question: What music is on your iPod today? Do you need to make some changes?

_____

_____

_____

_____

DAY 55

Can God help me overcome the impossible?

Today's Teen: David
Today's Action Verse: 1 Samuel 17:50
Storyline: 1 Samuel 17

David Speaks Today: *"By yourself, you are unmatched against the enemy. But with God, you can do anything."*

Digging Deeper: Goliath was not the cuddly giant we're used to seeing on VeggieTales or Sunday School flannel boards. He was a terrorist, bent on destroying all of Israel. Every day for six weeks, the army of Israel cowered in fear, knowing if the Philistines won the battle, they would lose their homes, their families, their jobs, and their country.

Enter David, the teen with the giant-sized faith in God, the young man who wasn't even supposed to be there. He stepped up to the challenge because nobody else would. God had taken care of him in the past, and he knew God would help him defeat this giant.

What giant do you face? Maybe you're suffering through the pain of your parents' divorce. Perhaps you have a habit you just can't seem to conquer. Or it may be a tough assignment at school that you can't seem to complete. Whatever your giant is, know that God is with you. When it seems that you don't have the strength, go with God, and He'll help you win your battles.

Just Like You: You'll probably never do hand-to-hand combat with a nine-foot giant like David did, but God will allow giants to come into your life. So how do you approach the seemingly impossible enemy? Here are the steps David took to victory:

- **Realize you can't win on your own strength.** David didn't think he was strong enough, smart enough, or athletic enough to beat Goliath. He knew it would be up to God to get the victory. David trusted God.
- **Don't listen to the doubters.** David's oldest brother was aggravated about him being there and questioned his motive. Saul thought David was crazy. And people will think you're crazy when you tell them that God can carry you through. David listened only to God.
- **Be yourself.** Saul's armor didn't work for David. So he worked with what he knew: his slingshot. David didn't try to impress Goliath—he couldn't. David came with what he had and trusted God to carry him through.
- **Reflect on past victories.** David never forgot the episodes with the lion and the bear. Remember the other hard times God got you through. Carry these memories as evidence of God's miracle-working power.

Did You Know? Goliath's armor weighed about 150 pounds, not counting the shield between his shoulders and shin armor. He stood about nine feet tall.

Today's Prayer: *God, I know it's impossible to fight the giants in my life and win without Your help. It is through Your strength that I can have the victory.*

Journal Question: What giants are you facing today? Are you facing them on your own or with God's power? How does God's power help?

_____

_____

_____

_____

_____

_____

_____

_____

Teen People of the Bible

DAY 56

What should I do when people doubt me?

Today's Teen: David
Today's Action Verse: 1 Samuel 17:37
Storyline: 1 Samuel 17

David Speaks Today: *"Don't listen to the negativity of the critics. Go for the dream God has put in your heart."*

Digging Deeper: When you take a leap of faith, you will have critics. That's guaranteed. David was no different. His eldest brother, questioning David's motives, was angry with him for his boldness and for even being at the battle. King Saul, who was supposed to be the leader, thought David was crazy to be willing to go toe-to-toe with Goliath. Maybe they weren't afraid that David would lose, but that he might win and show them up. They were supposed to be warriors: tall, tough, trained, and ready. Instead they were faithless cowards.

Don't be surprised when you face criticism, even from other Christians. Accusers may say you're being a little too radical. They may mock your willingness to share your faith. They'll be a little uncomfortable with your excitement about what's going on in your church and in your own spiritual life.

So you have a choice. You can listen to the doomsayers or ignore them. If you push on, God will do something great with your life. It's your choice.

Just Like You: Do you think you're the first one to get criticized for taking your walk with God to the next level, for having that radical faith that reaches for the impossible? Consider these ordinary people whom God asked to do pretty extraordinary things:

- **Gideon:** He was just minding his own business and wasn't even the best leader in his family. God asked him to fight Israel's fiercest enemy with only 300 men! Can you imagine the looks he got? His people must have thought, *God told you to do what?* But Gideon's weak faith became strong when he saw what God could do. (See Judges 6–7.)

- **Noah:** Building a boat is no big deal now, but in Noah's day it was as crazy as any idea that had ever been hatched. Even the concept of rain was new. It had never once rained down on the earth. And there Noah was, building a boat and taking 100 years to do it. But Noah believed God when others didn't and, in doing so, God saved Noah's family and the human race from the Flood. (See Genesis 6–8).

- **Hudson Taylor:** Taylor had a God-given passion to bring the love of God to China—an extreme calling, some might think. But Taylor's faith proved worthwhile. By the time he died, China Inland Mission had 205 mission stations, more than 800 missionaries, and 125,000 Chinese Christians.

- **Thomas Edison:** Thomas Edison didn't speak until he was almost four, but when he began speaking, he showed himself to be very inquisitive. Edison was in school only a short while; teachers said he was "addled" and thought that perhaps he wasn't very smart or capable. Only his mother believed that he could amount to anything. By the end of his life, he not only had invented a practical light bulb (after many trials), but also held more than 1,000 patents and had become America's greatest inventor.

- _____

And you can pencil your name in by the last bullet—because God is still in the business of taking our ordinary lives and weak faith and doing something completely extraordinary.

Did You Know? Goliath was covered head-to-toe in thick, impenetrable metal. The only exposed area of his body would likely have been his face, which is exactly where David cast the stone from his slingshot.

Today's Prayer: *Lord, give me the strength to resist the criticism of those who wish to see me fail.*

Journal Question: Who are the people who doubt you the most? How can you combat their criticism?

_____

_____

_____

_____

_____

_____

✥ ✥ ✥ ✥ ✥ ✥ ✥ ✥ ✥  ✥ ✥ ✥ ✥ ✥ ✥ ✥ ✥ ✥

Can a girlfriend or boyfriend bring me total happiness?

Today's Teen: Michal

Today's Action Verses: 1 Samuel 18:20; 1 Chronicles 15:29

Storyline: 1 Samuel 18:28–30; 19:8–18

Michal Speaks Today: _"Relationships are good, but don't be fooled into thinking that a relationship with the person of your dreams will satisfy all of your needs. Only God can do that."_

✥ ✥

Digging Deeper: The more she watched David, the more Michal, the daughter of King Saul, loved David. He was a rugged shepherd boy turned warrior who'd overcome all the odds and defeated Israel's worst enemy. As her father's fear and bitter hatred of David increased, even that couldn't extinguish her love.

David eventually passed Saul's tricky tests and married Michal, but the relationship didn't bring Michal lasting happiness.

Let me share with you what I perceive to be Michal's downfall: I believe her love grew beyond romance. It became an obsession. She worshipped David. And because she depended upon this relationship to bring her happiness, Michal became disappointed. David failed to fulfill her expectations. I think she grew from a lovesick young girl into a bitter old woman. The man she had looked to for happiness disappointed her and let her down.

Sadly, Michal was not the first or last person to be disappointed by life, by people, by love. That's why it's important to anchor yourself in Christ because He'll never let you down. He'll never fail you. You may find your one true love, but even the world's greatest soul mate will not satisfy all your needs.

Just Like You: How do you know if your relationship is bordering on the obsessive? Here are a few warning signs:

- **You spend every waking moment thinking about that person.** OK, maybe this is unfair, but try not to let your boyfriend or your girlfriend dominate your thinking.
- **Your time with him or her takes you away from important activities.** A good boyfriend or girlfriend will actually *help* you in your studies and your important activities.
- **You spend less time with God.** This is a really big red flag. If you notice that your quiet time is dwindling at the expense of late-night phone calls, it may be time to scale back your relationship and refocus your priorities.
- **You never talk about spiritual things.** OK, you don't have to have five-hour theological discussions, but if you can never comfortably talk about your relationship with God *together*, maybe something is wrong.
- **He or she encourages you to cross the line.** Are you being pushed to compromise your purity? If so, it's time to slam on the brakes!

Did You Know? Why did David have to kill 200 Philistines before he could marry Michal? (See 1 Samuel 18:17–27.)

A prospective groom customarily brought the bride's family a gift, a dowry—not as a way of buying a bride, but as compensation to the bride's parents for their loss of the daughter's service. Well, since David was poor and had no money for a dowry, Saul came up with this rather devious scheme, hoping David would be killed in the process.

Today's Prayer: *Dear God, help me to keep my perspective. I know You may lead me to love someone a lot—but I understand that no human relationship can replace the relationship I can have with You.*

Journal Question: Are you depending on a girlfriend or boyfriend for total happiness? If so, what can you do to change that and make God your first priority for happiness? What does the word *happiness* mean to you?

_____

_____

_____

_____

_____

_____

_____

_____

_____

_____

_____

_____

_____

_____

_____

_____

Does it matter who my friends are?

Today's Teen: David
Today's Action Verse: 1 Samuel 18:1
Storyline: 1 Samuel 18:1–5

David Speaks Today: *"A good friend who will stick by you and support your values is a priceless treasure. Hold on to your good friends."*

Digging Deeper: Jonathan was a great choice of friend for David. Jonathan was not just a cool guy to hang out with, but he also shared David's values. They both wanted to do big things for God, and they stuck by each other's side through thick and thin.

Their friendship prospered in spite of their differences. Jonathan was from a royal family. His dad was the king. As a prince, he probably had servants and people who tended to his every need. This young man could have whatever he wanted. On the other hand, David was not of royal descent; he was just a shepherd boy, who was apparently not even well liked by his own family.

The friendship built on trust can overcome differences in color, income levels, and backgrounds—it can overcome many differences. What matters, though, is that friends share the same values.

You should be picky when it comes to choosing your friends. I believe David was. David needed a real friend—someone to stick by him, someone who likewise honored God and would help him grow closer to God. And Jonathan was that friend.

Just Like You: What are some things you should look for in a friend? Here are some helpful tips:

- **Choose friends who share your faith.** The Bible says not to be unequally yoked with unbelievers (2 Corinthians 6:14).
- **Choose friends who are willing to tell you, in a loving and sincere way, when you're wrong.** In Proverbs 27:17, this type of relationship is described as iron sharpening iron.
- **Choose friends who will encourage and build you up** instead of tear you down (1 Thessalonians 5:11).
- **Choose friends who will be loyal and not gossip about you,** not tell your personal information to everyone at school or church.
- **Choose friends who share some common interests with you, but also challenge you with new ideas and new thoughts.**
- **Choose friends who encourage you to do the right things,** such as obey your parents, stay pure, go to church, and listen to your teachers.

Did You Know? A Southern Baptist Council on Family Life study revealed that 88 percent of the children raised in evangelical homes leave church at the age of 18, never to return.

Today's Prayer: *God, please give me wisdom to choose good friends—and the courage to stay away from people who might have a negative influence on me.*

Journal Question: Do any of your friends seem to be dragging you down? How can you gracefully put a safe distance between them and you to prevent that effect?

_____

_____

_____

_____

_____

_____

_____

DAY 59

Can one person really make a difference?

Today's Teen: Jonathan
Today's Action Verse: 1 Samuel 14:6
Storyline: 1 Samuel 14:1–15

Jonathan Speaks Today: *"When you trust God, you can do things that seem humanly impossible."*

Digging Deeper: Unlike his cowardly father and the rest of the generals and soldiers, Jonathan was not one to sit back and accept defeat. He wasn't sure his attack would be successful, but he wanted to go down trying.

Radical faith—this was a theme in Jonathan's life. Like his best friend, David, he didn't see obstacles, giants, or armies—he only saw God's ability to defeat the enemy.

One man, one woman—that's who God is looking for. Jonathan understood the incredible power of one young person who answers the call and steps out in faith.

The good news is that you don't have to be a prince, like Jonathan, to do something great. You don't need wealthy parents. You don't need famous relatives. You don't even need good looks or athletic talent. All you need is passion and heart—passion for God and a heart for His people.

Will you be the *one*?

Just Like You: Jeremy Blaschke, a 17-year-old in Clovis, New Mexico, who was running for president of his homeschool association, was in need of a service project to support his pro-life campaign platform. As he glanced over Focus on the Family's Web site, information about Option Ultrasound caught his attention. Option Ultrasound is a Focus on the Family initiative that helps provide ultrasound machines for crisis pregnancy centers. These centers help unwed mothers make tough decisions. Statistics show that the majority of abortion-minded mothers choose life when they see an ultrasound of their baby.

As Jeremy read about the potential for these ultrasound machines to save lives, an idea clicked: *We could just buy one.* So Jeremy and his team launched a campaign to raise $25,000—enough for one machine. Raffles, presentations, and events were organized and carried out, and the team, which had expanded to 30 young people, exceeded their goal. After a year's work, they raised more than $33,000 dollars. Jeremy and a few of his team members went to Focus on the Family to present the money to James Dobson.

The effort was about more than money: "It was about saving life," Jeremy said. (Cheryl Wilhelmi, www.breakawaymag.com, www.briomag.com).

Did You Know? Jonathan and his armor bearer beat back an entire garrison of Philistine soldiers. A garrison usually contained about 250 men. So two poorly armed soldiers were victorious against 250 of the world's finest warriors!

Today's Prayer: *God, help me to make a difference in my family, my school, my church, and my community. I'm only one person, but I know You can empower me to do things that seem impossible.*

Journal Question: In what situations can you make a difference? Is today the day that God wants you to step up to the plate? What will you do? Write your action plans below.

_____

_____

_____

_____

_____

_____

_____

✛ ✛ ✛ ✛ ✛ ✛ ✛ ✛ ✛ ✛   ✛ ✛ ✛ ✛ ✛ ✛ ✛ ✛ ✛ ✛

What happens if I'm not sure of God's will?

Today's Teen: Jonathan
Today's Action Verse: 1 Samuel 14:6
Storyline: 1 Samuel 14:1–15

Jonathan Speaks Today: *"Life is full of risks, but don't let fear of failure immobilize you. If you step out, you can be sure that God will guide your way."*

✛ ✛

Digging Deeper: You've got to love the short pep talk Jonathan gave his young armor bearer before they launched their risky, two-man sneak attack on the enemy. Notice Jonathan was not certain what the outcome would be and stated, *"It may be that [perhaps (NIV)] the Lord will work for us"* (1 Samuel 14:6). That's interesting.

Jonathan wasn't waiting for an absolute, fire-from-heaven, thunderous yes from the Almighty. A need presented itself, and two willing people, Jonathan and his armor bearer, grabbed the rare opportunity.

This is real life. Rarely in life will you have absolute, risk-free, bank-on-it type of assurance from the Lord before you're about to embark on something life changing. God works through open doors and opportunities. He doesn't want us to spend endless hours of speculation: *Should I do this? Should I not do this? What should I do?* This is sometimes called "paralysis by analysis." Jonathan didn't suffer from that; he didn't hedge. He seized the opportunity and let God sort out the details.

Life is full of risks. It's better to do something and make a mistake than to do nothing at all. Churches are filled with trembling souls afraid to mess up.

Be a person of action. Walk through open doors. Take golden opportunities. Make decisions, and follow through. Along the way, God will show you where to go, just like He did Jonathan.

Just Like You: Brandy was overwhelmed by a dozen glossy college catalogs spread out across her kitchen table. The application deadlines were fast approaching, and she had to make some decisions. She couldn't apply for them all. She really wanted to do God's will, but He wasn't exactly writing the name of the right college on the wall.

Brandy's dad sat across from her with a sheet of paper. At the top, he wrote the name of the 12 schools she liked the most. Then he asked Brandy about the pros and cons of each one. The college her dad attended would give her a partial alumni scholarship, but none of her friends were going there. Then there was the school two of her closest girlfriends had chosen, but this school didn't have a strong nursing program, a curriculum of interest to Brandy. Brandy and her dad had this discussion about each of the 12 schools. After a few hours, they were able to narrow the list to five strong possibilities. She would apply to each one. Then they prayed and asked God to open the right doors and close the wrong ones.

Did You Know? Jonathan was no stranger to battle. He fought alongside his father, Saul, in many of Israel's wars. The name *Jonathan* means "God has given" or "gift of God."

Today's Prayer: *Help me to be a person of action and not of hesitation. Help me to walk through open doors and make the most of opportunities.*

Journal Question: What spiritual risks are you afraid to take? How can you overcome your fears and take the risks for God?

_____

_____

_____

_____

_____

DAY 61

Why should I be loyal to my friends?

Today's Teen: Jonathan
Today's Action Verse: John 15:13
Storyline: 1 Samuel 18:1–4; 23:16–18

Jonathan Speaks Today: *"Loyalty is the most important part of friendship."*

Digging Deeper: Jonathan understood what it meant to be a loyal friend. He was there for David through thick and thin. He even gave up the chance to be the next king because he knew God wanted David to be on the throne. Jonathan's friendship saw David through some of the toughest times of his life.

Loyalty is what friendship is all about. After David defeated Goliath, David quickly became a celebrity. Everyone wanted a piece of him. But Jonathan wasn't a fair-weather friend. He wasn't David's friend because David was popular. Jonathan loved David for who he was inside.

What kind of friend are you? Are you willing to stick up for the people you care about, even if it means suffering a little? Are you there when you're needed the most? Are you a listening ear and a shoulder to cry on? Will you defend your friends against gossip?

Jonathan knew that to have a good friend required *being* a good friend.

Just Like You: So what exactly does it take to be a good friend? An unknown author provides a good answer to that question:

The A–Z of Friendship

A Friend:

(A)ccepts you as you are

(B)elieves in you

(C)alls you just to say "Hi"

(D)oesn't give up on you

(E)nvisions the whole of you (even the unfinished parts)

(F)orgives your mistakes

(G)ives unconditionally

(H)elps you

(I)nvites you over

(J)ust likes to be with you

(K)eeps you close at heart

(L)oves you for who you are

(M)akes a difference in your life

(N)ever judges

(O)ffers support

(P)icks you up

(Q)uiets your fears

(R)aises your spirits

(S)ays nice things about you

(T)ells you the truth when you need to hear it

(U)nderstands you

(V)alues you

(W)alks beside you

(X)-plains things you don't understand

(Y)ells when you won't listen and

(Z)aps you back to reality

—Author unknown ✛

Did You Know? When Jonathan gave David his robe and his sword, it was a powerful symbol of acceptance. To receive this gift from a prince was considered the highest honor in society. Some experts think that Jonathan actually gave up the opportunity to be the next king with this gesture.

Today's Prayer: *God, give me wisdom in choosing the right friends and help me to be loyal to my friends.*

Journal Question: Do you stand by your friends when others criticize them? How can you show loyalty to your friends?

_____

_____

_____

_____

_____

_____

_____

_____

_____

_____

_____

_____

_____

_____

_____

_____

_____

_____

_____

_____

_____

_____

✢ ✤ ✢ ✤ ✢ ✤ ✢ ✤ ✢ ✤   ✤ ✢ ✤ ✢ ✤ ✢ ✤ ✢ ✤

Does God have a plan for me even if my parents don't follow Him?

Today's Teen: Jonathan
Today's Action Verse: 1 Samuel 18:1
Storyline: 1 Samuel 18:1 through 19:6

Jonathan Speaks Today: *"You should love and honor your parents, but if they lead you into sin, you should make the choice to do right."*

✤ ✢ ✤ ✢ ✤ ✢ ✤ ✢ ✤ ✢ ✤ ✢ ✤ ✢ ✤ ✢ ✤ ✢ ✤ ✢ ✤ ✢

Digging Deeper: Like most young people, Jonathan learned a lot from watching his father, Saul. Unfortunately, Saul was one of those fathers who, by example, taught his children what *not to do.* Saul should have been the most courageous man in Israel. After all, he was selected to be king because he was a choice young man of great physical stature. But Saul's faith was shallow. When the people looked for a leader, Saul was nowhere to be found. When Goliath challenged the army of Israel, Saul shrunk from the fight. When challenged by David's popularity among the people, Saul feared David. (See 1 Samuel 10:21; 17:11; 18:12.)

Jonathan chose to be different from his father. While he respected Saul, he knew there was a better way to live—God's way.

It may be this way with you. Maybe your parents don't take faith very seriously. Or maybe they aren't Christians at all. But their mistakes don't have to keep you from going places with God. You can be different if you choose.

Just Like You: Each Sunday in church, Jack got a bad feeling as he noticed all the intact, seemingly perfect families there. How he wished his dad would come to at least one service. But his dad would rather spend his off days at the casino.

Jack loved his dad very much and wanted him to know the Lord. But deep down, Jack had a real fear that he was destined to repeat his father's mistakes. That's what his mother and the rest of his family always told him: "Jack, you're going to end up just like your dad."

Every time those doubts crept into his mind, Jack remembered the words of Jeremiah 29:11. He also remembered the reassurances of his youth leader: "Jack, God has plans for you—they are your plans, not your father's, not your family's, but God's will for you."

Knowing that God has a future planned for you and that you don't have to repeat your parents' mistakes brings relief and peace.

Did You Know? Because of Saul's sin, Jonathan lost the opportunity to become Israel's next king. It would be through David's line that God would bring the King of kings, Jesus, the Messiah.

Today's Prayer: *God, help me honor my parents and follow them when they obey You, and help me make wise decisions and choices for myself when they don't obey You.*

Journal Question: What mistakes and sins of your parents are you tempted to repeat? How can you avoid making these mistakes?

_____

_____

_____

_____

_____

_____

_____

Teen People of the Bible

✝ ✢ ✝ ✚ ✝ ✚ ✝ ✚ ✝ ✢   ✝ ✢ ✝ ✚ ✝ ✚ ✝ ✚ ✝ ✢

Is it OK to come in second if I've tried my best?

Today's Teen: Jonathan
Today's Action Verse: 1 Samuel 18:1, 4
Storyline: 1 Samuel 18

Jonathan Speaks Today: *"It takes real courage to admit that someone else is better at something than you are."*

✝ ✢ ✝ ✚ ✝ ✚ ✝ ✚ ✝ ✢ ✝ ✚ ✝ ✚ ✝ ✚ ✝ ✢ ✝ ✚ ✝ ✚ ✝ ✢

Digging Deeper: When Jonathan, the prince and heir to the throne, acknowledged God's plan to have David be Israel's next king, it was a rare and incredible sacrifice. Jesus said, *"Greater love hath no man than this, that a man lay down his life for his friends"* (John 15:13).

Why did Jonathan do this? Why would he settle for second fiddle? How could he watch someone else take a spot he could so easily have had? Why wasn't Jonathan selfish?

The answer, I propose, is that Jonathan lived to serve others, especially those closest to him. He gave up the right to be king because he could see God's plan unfolding in the life of David. To give up everything and play second fiddle takes a real friend—a loyal friend.

We live in a world that says backstabbing, betrayal, and deceit are OK if that's what it takes to get to the top. If you watch TV long enough, you'll think that it's OK to gossip about your friends; you'll think it's fine to spread rumors that hurt them; you'll think it's a sign of weakness to put others first.

But as a believer, you can be a difference maker by putting your friends first. Your kindness and love can shine as a bright light in a dark world.

Just Like You: Angela was busy working on her algebra homework one night when the phone rang.

Her mom came into her room and said, "Ang, it's Jess!"

Angela picked up the receiver, "Hey, what's up?"

"Did you hear about Ronny?"

"No, what happened?"

"I just heard what really happened last week with Alice."

Angela's stomach tightened. Ronny and Alice both were her good friends.

"Well, I don't really think we should be talking...."

"Well, I haven't told anyone—just you."

Angela hedged, "Yeah, I like Ronny...and Alice, and I think we should give them the benefit of the doubt."

"Well, don't you want to know, so you can pray?"

Angela prayed a silent prayer. "Jess, I just don't want to talk about this. I think I should hear it from them first."

Did You Know? Author and preacher Henry Ward Beecher said, "Every man should keep a fair-sized cemetery in which to bury the faults of his friends."

Today's Prayer: *Dear Lord, help me to be a servant to others, even if this means giving up for someone else something that is important to me.*

Journal Question: Why do you think playing second fiddle is so hard? How can you overcome these feelings?

_____

_____

_____

_____

_____

_____

_____

Why do I feel badly when God blesses me instead of other people?

Today's Teen: Solomon

Today's Action Verses: 1 Kings 2:23–25

Storyline: 1 Kings 1 and 2:13–25

Solomon Speaks Today: *"If God gives you a big opportunity, don't be surprised if some of your friends and family are jealous."*

Digging Deeper: High drama occurred when David chose Solomon as Israel's next king. Solomon's older brother, Adonijah, being the elder son, thought himself more qualified to be king. Actually, I think Adonijah was power-hungry and wanted the unlimited perks that come with being king. But God clearly wanted Solomon on the throne even though he was still young.

After an elaborate conspiracy, during which Adonijah tried to get his own priest, his own general, and even his own false queen, David stepped in and made Solomon king.

God clearly had His hand on Solomon and had chosen him to be in this position of leadership, but it didn't come without some tough trials along the way.

If you are ever given an opportunity like Solomon was given, don't be surprised if others get pretty jealous. And don't be surprised if the jealous people are supposedly your friends. Solomon's own brother tried to sidestep him.

You can't let others' jealousy or pride get in the way of God's will for your life. So shake it off, and remember that you live for an audience of One—God.

Just Like You: During Greg's sophomore year, auditions for the lead role in the annual Christmas production were being held. Greg had always loved drama and really enjoyed taking theater, so he was quite interested in auditioning. Greg had a pretty good friend, Gavin, who was also interested. So they both tried out for the same part.

Every Thursday for three weeks, Greg, Gavin, and four other students tried out for the role. Finally, decision day came. The last day of auditions, they sat in the auditorium and awaited the drama teacher's decision. After congratulating everyone on his efforts, she announced that Greg had won the part.

The other candidates seemed to be happy for Greg—except for Gavin. He stomped out of the room even before Greg had a chance to say anything. Greg felt terrible. He wanted this part, but not if it meant losing his friend.

It got worse. The next day, a few more of Greg's friends refused to talk to him. He wondered why. Then one of them told him what Gavin had said. The rumor was that Greg's father had made a financial contribution to the school's performing arts fund, and that was why the drama teacher awarded Greg the part.

None of this was true, but still the lie seemed to stick with many of Greg's closest friends. He felt betrayed, hurt, and angry.

Did You Know? David had ruled Israel for 33 years, and the throne would normally go to his oldest son, but God gave David wisdom and told him that Solomon should be king. For this to happen, David actually had to appoint Solomon as king while David, himself, was still alive.

Today's Prayer: *God, help me to stay humble when You give me special opportunities. And help me to forgive those who are jealous of where You have brought me in my life.*

Journal Question: Do you have a friend who just seems to get all the coolest stuff? How does that make you feel? Have you ever been shown favor over a friend? How did that make you feel?

_____

_____

_____

_____

_____

_____

_____

_____

_____

_____

✛ ✛ ✛ ✛ ✛ ✛ ✛ ✛ ✛ ✛ ✛ ✛ ✛ ✛ ✛ ✛ ✛ ✛ ✛

Am I living off my parents' faith?

Today's Teen: Solomon
Today's Action Verse: 1 Chronicles 28:9
Storyline: 1 Chronicles 28–29

Solomon Speaks Today: *"A spiritual life isn't automatic. You can't live off your parent's faith. You have to make your own choices."*

✛ ✛

Digging Deeper: Solomon was young, maybe in his teens, when David died and basically gave Solomon the keys to the kingdom. There were great expectations of Solomon as king of Israel. His father passed on to him great wealth and wise counsel. On top of that, God gave Solomon great wisdom, insight, and wealth as he prepared to lead God's people, Israel. God placed leadership in Solomon's hands and a promise to establish his kingdom forever if he continued to follow the Lord's commandments and judgments.

As David approached death, he gave young Solomon one very specific instruction: *Know God for yourself.* Solomon couldn't live off of his father's faith. Faith isn't automatically passed on from generation to generation. Each new generation must make the choice, must take the baton and run with it.

If you have Christian parents and have grown up in church, that fact doesn't mean you will naturally serve God. You still have to make your own choice.

Maybe you feel pressure from everyone around you to commit yourself to God. Maybe your parent or other Christian leaders wonder why you struggle with temptation. Don't feel like you're a failure. Your choice to follow God is just as difficult as the choice is for someone who is new to Christianity.

Take David's deathbed advice seriously. Get to know God personally—in your own way.

Just Like You: David's wise advice to Solomon is advice that can help you live a successful life right now. It is basically broken down into five nuggets of wisdom. You may want to post this list on your mirror or put it on your refrigerator:

1. **Get to know God personally.** You can't do anything without God's strength. You can't walk the Christian walk without knowing Him and having Him as your guide.
2. **Learn God's commands.** His boundaries aren't rules for a no-fun lifestyle. They are guardrails for the road of life to keep you on the path to success.
3. **Worship God with a clean heart.** Confession isn't just good for the soul—it breaks down the barrier of sin that keeps you from loving God at your fullest. Don't hide your sin; bring it before God.
4. **Be faithful.** If you've signed your name to something, stick it out. Be dependable. Be trustworthy. Be true to your word.
5. **Don't stay discouraged.** Some days you'll want to give up on the whole spiritual walk. When hard times come, look up for encouragement and look into God's Word for fresh strength.

Did You Know? David was given the blueprint for the temple in a vision, during which he copied down every specific detail. David then gave this plan to Solomon, who was to build the temple according to these very important criteria.

Today's Prayer: *God, I want to know You for who You are. I don't want to just try to get by on my parents' faith.*

Journal Question: Are you doing all this Christian stuff because you have to—because your parents make you do it? Or have you made your own choice about faith? If you have made your own choice, describe how it happened.

_____

_____

_____

_____

_____

_____

_____

_____

_____

_____

_____

_____

_____

_____

_____

_____

_____

If God calls me, will God equip me?

Today's Teen: Solomon
Today's Action Verses: 1 Chronicles 28:5–7
Storyline: 1 Chronicles 28

Solomon Speaks Today: *"If God calls you to something great, He'll equip you to do the job."*

Digging Deeper: Imagine the pressure on young Solomon. The entire weight of God's people was on him—all while he was still struggling with issues just like you struggle with today. But God had His hand on Solomon.

Fortunately, God didn't call Solomon to do a job without equipping him. David, Solomon's father, had stored up a lot of money so Solomon could build the temple. David had prepared the people for this job. He'd defeated the enemies of Israel so Solomon could establish the kingdom in peace.

Maybe you feel a bit overwhelmed in your current situation. Questions arise about your future: *Will I get into college? What kind of career will I have? Where is God calling me? What if I mess up?*

Here's some encouragement: If God calls you, God will equip you. He never sends His people unprepared. You can rest easy in knowing that whatever challenges lie ahead, God will not only be there with you, but He'll also give you the gifts and resources you need to succeed.

Solomon wouldn't have to lead Israel alone, and you won't have to face your future alone either.

Just Like You: As Chase sat down to take his SAT exams, his palms grew sweaty. He could feel the little hairs sticking up on the back of his neck. Goose bumps were beginning to form all across his arms. This was the big day—the big test.

He had to score high. Otherwise, his parents would "kill" him, his teachers would be disappointed, and he would be a bad role model for his younger sister. Chase tried to concentrate; he didn't do well when he was nervous.

Chase then mouthed a silent prayer: *God, I'm so nervous. I don't know how I'm going to do this. I studied hard, but I'm afraid I'm going to forget everything.*

A warm sense of relief washed over Chase. He knew the test would still be hard, but he knew, too, that God would be there with him no matter what the outcome. He remembered David's words to Solomon, spoken thousands of years ago: *"Be strong and of good courage, and do it: fear not, nor be dismayed, for the LORD God, even my God, will be with thee; he will not fail thee, nor forsake thee"* (1 Chronicles 28:20).

Did You Know? US teens have some strange beliefs. According to the Barna Group, slightly more than half believe that Jesus committed sins while he was on earth. About 60 percent think that a good person can earn eternal salvation through good deeds. Only 9 percent of self-described born-again teens believe that moral truth is absolute.

Today's Prayer: *God, give me strength and courage to tackle whatever lies in my future.*

Journal Question: What responsibility or activity scares you the most? What reassurance do you have from God that He'll go with you?

_____

_____

_____

_____

_____

_____

Why is it important to grow up?

Today's Teen: Solomon
Today's Action Verses: 1 Kings 2:1–2
Storyline: 1 Kings 2:1–9

Solomon Speaks Today: *"There is a time in every young person's life when he or she has to step up and act like a man or a woman."*

Digging Deeper: David had dreamed of building the Temple, but God told this aging king that He would give this huge job to David's son, Solomon. Solomon was still in his teens, but God wanted him to be king and start a whole new chapter in Israel's history.

Solomon had to step up to the plate and lead. He couldn't afford to be immature at this important moment in his life. Millions of people would now look to him for leadership and wisdom.

So you're not going to be a king anytime soon, but you're probably feeling similar to Solomon. Big things are ahead of you: college, a career, adulthood. You will have to step up and act like an adult instead of a kid. That doesn't mean you can't ever have a good time or laugh anymore. Maturity simply means that you're stepping up from being a kid to being a servant leader.

Your world needs you to step up to the plate: Young people need a positive role model. Lost people need to hear about the Savior. Needy people could use your service.

Just Like You: Sweating through the brutal wind sprints during preseason conditioning drills, Phil was tempted to slow down a bit. The cramps in his side, the heaviness in his legs, and his aching back told him to let up a bit. He really had nothing to lose. His starting position was clearly locked in.

But Phil was also a captain and a senior. He was expected to be a leader on the team. The freshmen watched him. If he slacked, they might slack. If he talked badly about the coach in the locker room, they might not think they had to listen to Coach. If he blew off classes, they might think they could blow them off too.

So Phil sucked in some air and kept running. It was time for Phil to be a leader. That particular day, being a leader meant pushing a little harder so the rest of the guys would keep pushing. Other days, it meant being a little more mature than he had been last year; it meant trying to stay out of trouble so he wouldn't lead the younger guys astray. Choosing to be a leader meant Phil was growing up.

Did You Know? Several sources state it took seven or seven and a half years to build the Temple; and Scriptures tell us Solomon put 153,600 men to work on the project (2 Chronicles 2:2, 17–18).

Today's Prayer: *God, help me to be a leader in my school, my community, and my family.*

Journal Question: In what way can you demonstrate maturity today? How can you be an example to younger believers, who may be looking up to you?

_____

_____

_____

_____

_____

_____

_____

_____

_____

Can I be confident and still be humble?

Today's Teen: Solomon
Today's Action Verse: 1 Kings 3:7
Storyline: 1 Kings 3:7–10

Solomon Speaks Today: *"Weakness before God is the key to success. Humility brings honor."*

Digging Deeper: If a modern psychologist had Solomon on the couch, he might say this young king was suffering from a lack of self-esteem. After all, if you read this young man's words, you might think he was a bit down. But Solomon wasn't depressed. He was actually very confident, but not in himself. Solomon had unlimited confidence in God. He knew he couldn't lead Israel by himself. He was only a young man following in the footsteps of his father, a great, popular, and wise king.

Solomon discovered a spiritual secret: humility is the key to success. That may sound a little strange, considering what you hear most people say today. How often have you heard that putting yourself first is the only way to get ahead? How often have you been told you have to look out for number one? But self-promotion is really the kiss of death when it comes to real spiritual success.

The moment you realize that you can do nothing *without* God and everything *with* God is the moment you put yourself on the pathway to success.

Just Like You: Just what is humility? It's been given a bad rap lately. You're probably thinking of a droopy, poorly dressed Christian with a constant frown and a woe-is-me attitude. But that's really not a picture of humility. You don't have to be Eeyore to be humble.

Let's look at what some famous Christians have had to say about humility:

- **Charles Spurgeon, famous preacher in England in the 1800s:** "Humility is to make a right estimate of one's self; it is no humility for a man to think less of himself than he ought."
- **John Wooden, championship basketball coach of UCLA Bruins:** "Talent is God-given; be humble."
- **John Newton, former slave trader and author of "Amazing Grace":** "I am persuaded that love and humility are the highest attainments in the school of Christ and the brightest evidences that He is indeed our Master."
- **C. S. Lewis, author of "The Chronicles of Narnia" series:** "Do not imagine that if you meet a really humble man he will be what most people call 'humble' nowadays: he will not be a sort of greasy, smarmy person, who is always telling you that, of course, he is nobody. Probably all you will think about him is that he seemed a cheerful, intelligent chap who took a real interest in what *you* said to *him*. If you do dislike him, it will be because you feel a little envious of anyone who seems to enjoy life so easily. He will not be thinking about humility: he will not be thinking about himself at all."

Did You Know? Solomon's temple was built on the same mountain range, Moriah, where Abraham offered Isaac. On this same hill, thousands of years later, is where Jesus Christ would be offered as the final sacrifice for sin.

Today's Prayer: *Dear Lord, please develop in me confidence and humility. I want to give You the credit for my successes, not claim it for myself.*

Journal Question: What does it really mean to be "weak before God"? How can you be humble and yet confident?

_____

_____

_____

_____

_____

What's the big deal about wisdom?

Today's Teen: Solomon
Today's Action Verses: 2 Chronicles 1:7; 1 Kings 3:9
Storyline: 1 Kings 3:1–15; 2 Chronicles 1:1–13

Solomon Speaks Today: *"Begin each day with a quest for wisdom, because wisdom will touch every other area of your life."*

✠ ✠ ✠ ✠ ✠ ✠ ✠ ✠ ✠ ✠ ✠ ✠ ✠ ✠ ✠ ✠ ✠ ✠

Digging Deeper: If you had one wish and a promise from God that it would be fulfilled, for what would you wish? Young Solomon had this rare opportunity. God basically told him he could have whatever he wanted.

What did Solomon choose? You might think he'd have picked money, a beautiful girlfriend, or a brand-new car (OK, chariot). But Solomon didn't pick any of those. He chose wisdom.

Now that sounds kind of lame, doesn't it? Solomon may have known that wisdom is the wellspring of life—the secret of success; but he, for sure, knew it was something he needed in his new role as king of Israel.

The world says that knowledge is power. Wisdom is much more than that. Wisdom is not only *knowing* what to do but also *having the courage* to do it. Knowledge can come from anywhere. Wisdom comes from God Almighty.

Solomon trusted that if he had wisdom, the rest of his life would fall into place. This was a young man who seemed to have his priorities in order.

The cool news is that God says anyone can have wisdom and as much as you are willing to ask for. So start your wisdom quest now.

Just Like You: So what exactly is wisdom? Is it the mind-numbing brilliance of Albert Einstein? If that were the case, then most of us would be left out. But God says anyone who wants wisdom can have it (James 1:5). Wisdom is not just book smarts. Wisdom is putting into practice God's pattern for life. It's knowing what to do and then doing it. Proverbs 3–4 (written by Solomon, by the way) identifies several characteristics and activities of the wise.

These are some of the characteristics of a person who is wise:
- Is loyal to God, family, and friends
- Is genuinely kind
- Trusts in the Lord and His will
- Puts God first
- Flees evil
- Is a good listener
- Has the character to do what's right

Did You Know? Solomon spoke 3,000 proverbs and wrote 1,005 songs (1 Kings 4:32).

Today's Prayer: *Dear Lord, give me wisdom so I can know You better and make the best choices in life.*

Journal Question: What can you do to obtain more of God's wisdom today?

_____

_____

_____

_____

_____

_____

_____

_____

_____

Is it wrong to be rich?

Today's Teen: Solomon
Today's Action Verse: 1 Kings 3:13
Storyline: 1 Kings 3:11–15; 1 Kings 10:14–29

Solomon Speaks Today: *"If God blesses you with a lot of money, make sure you don't let it change your perspective on life. Use it to help others."*

Digging Deeper: Even though Solomon asked for wisdom, God decided to bless him with great wealth too. He wasn't just rich—he was filthy rich.

Some people teach that it's wrong to be rich; others teach that God wants you to be rich. Well, neither of these opinions is really what the Bible says. In fact, the Apostle Paul said, *"I know both how to be abased, and I know how to abound: everywhere and in all things I am instructed both to be full and to be hungry, both to abound and to suffer need"* (Philippians 4:12). We could say it this way: If God makes me rich, great. If God makes me poor, OK. Either way, I'm happy.

God made Solomon rich. God may make you rich someday. Or you may be poor. What's important is not what is in your wallet but what is in your heart. What matters is not whether you have abundance but that you use whatever resources God gives to help others find peace with Him.

Just Like You: You don't have to hang around church people very long to hear the word *tithe.* What's this all about?

Tithing is giving God a portion of what He's given you. Most Bible teachers believe that 10 percent is a good starting point. A tithe was a practice established by Abraham (Genesis 14:20) even before God gave Israel the law. So it's not something you *have* to do, but something you *should* do—something you should *want* to do (2 Corinthians 9:7).

Giving shouldn't be drudgery—it's a privilege. You'll find the more you give, the better you will feel about yourself. It's an expression of your love for God and all He's given you.

God doesn't look at the size of your tithes and offerings, but the direction of your heart. God doesn't look at the size of your bank account, but the priorities of your spending habits. Do you horde your money for yourself, or are you a generous giver?

Did You Know? Solomon may have been one of the richest men *in history*. Scholars debate this, but many believe he was wealthier than even some of today's billionaires, if his net worth were adjusted for inflation, standard of living, and so on.

Today's Prayer: *God, help me to look at my money as a gift from You and not my own. I want to be a giver—a generous giver—who looks out for the needs of others.*

Journal Question: How does the amount of money a person has affect your attitude towards that person?

_____

_____

_____

_____

_____

_____

_____

_____

_____

_____

Why did Solomon have so many wives?

Today's Teen: Solomon
Today's Action Verse: Nehemiah 13:26
Storyline: 1 Kings 11:1–13

Solomon Speaks Today: *"God's plan has always been for marriage between one man and one woman. Let me tell you, any other way brings trouble and heartache."*

Digging Deeper: Solomon began his life with wisdom. And because of his father's faithfulness and God's blessing, he had such promise. He had the potential to accomplish more than any other leader in Israel's history.

But while Solomon led Israel to greatness in size, strength, and influence, his heart was gradually turned away from God. Bible teacher Warren Wiersbe has this to say: "Solomon's heart was not right with God ([1 Kings] 11:4). God wanted 'integrity of heart' (9:4), which means a united heart single to the glory of God. But Solomon had a divided heart—he loved the world as he tried to serve God" (*Wiersbe's Expository Outlines on the Old Testament*).

Solomon's life shows us that, even when you start out with wisdom, you're never out of the danger zone. You never reach a point where sin is OK—no matter what position you're in, no matter how much God blesses you, no matter how much money you have. Veering outside of God's moral guardrails always leads to bitter consequences.

Just Like You: So are you still scratching your head about Solomon? Are you wondering why he had 1,000 wives?

Many of Solomon's marriages were the results of agreements or treaties he made with other countries. It sounds a bit weird, but Solomon would marry the daughter of another king so the two countries could be allies. Polygamy (the practice of having more than one wife) was not only legal, but common. Yet it still went against God's original plan as described in Genesis 2:24.

Solomon's many marriages helped him build Israel into the world's richest and most powerful country, but they also led him away from the Lord. He began worshipping other gods—the gods of his wives—something his father, David, would never have done.

In the end, Solomon's moral compromises resulted in short-term pleasures but long-term heartaches. God's plan for sex and relationships has always been marriage between one man and one woman (Genesis 2:18–24).

So why did God allow Solomon and others in the Bible to have more than one wife? Could it be He allowed it to illustrate just how miserable a man or woman would be when living outside of God's plan? But it is important to note that God had grace—the same grace He extends to us when we fail Him.

Did You Know? Solomon built Israel into a military power, according to *The Teacher's Commentary* by L. and L. O. Richards: "He fortified key cities on the perimeter of Israel's territory and set up outer command posts to give early warning of possible enemy military buildups. In addition, Solomon developed a strong and mobile strike force, assembling some 1,400 chariots and 12,000 horsemen, and building stables for 4,000 horses. Solomon's chariot cities have been excavated and indicate the extent of the large standing army the king maintained."

Today's Prayer: *God, I want to commit to saving myself for marriage—and to being faithful to that future bride or groom You have for me. I want to learn the lesson of Solomon, avoid his sin, and follow Your will for my life.*

Journal Question: What are some potential "danger zones" of temptation for you?

_____

_____

_____

_____

_____

_____

_____

_____

_____

_____

Is a life without God worth anything?

Today's Teen: Solomon
Today's Action Verses: Ecclesiastes 1:2; 12:13–14
Storyline: Ecclesiastes

Solomon Speaks Today: *"What you do for God is the only thing that matters in your life."*

Digging Deeper: How many times have you watched a documentary about a famous Hollywood celebrity, only to be disappointed by how miserable that person seemed to be? Well, this was Solomon. He had it all—wealth, power, women, fame. He was the most popular person in the entire world. Nobody compared with him in intellect, riches, and leadership. And yet, his memoirs in Ecclesiastes reveal a cynical, lonely, miserable man. Solomon discovered that nothing in this world satisfies. Everything fades away. There is no lasting glory in what this world offers.

It's hard to believe this, especially when it seems that happiness is just a job, a college degree, or a few thousand dollars away. It's easy to think that money and popularity can bring joy, but they really can't.

The only joy is in knowing Jesus Christ. The only satisfaction is found in serving Him. Our home isn't really here on earth, but in heaven.

This doesn't mean you have to live a life of poverty. It doesn't mean God hates rich people. But happiness and satisfaction cannot be bought with money. It can't be found in relationships. It won't be realized with power. Only God satisfies.

Just Like You: As a popular teen actor, Kirk Cameron made $50,000 a week, drove fancy sports cars, traveled around the world, and was flooded with offers as a lead in big-budget movies. But inside, Kirk felt empty. Despite all of his success, it seemed something was missing. He had everything he'd ever wanted, yet he lacked something money couldn't buy.

A friend asked Kirk to his church in Fullerton, California. There, the preacher shared a message about God's holiness, judgment against sin, and the concepts of grace, mercy, and the Cross. Through the death, burial, and resurrection of Christ, Kirk could have peace with God. Kirk went home and pondered the preacher's words.

A few weeks later, while pulled off on the side of the road, Kirk prayed a clumsy prayer and asked God to show him that He was real. Kirk's prayer was answered not with any miraculous sign but with a very real sense that God heard him—that He was listening to him.

Now Kirk Cameron uses his talents to share this same message about God and Christ with others. Besides acting in the popular *Left Behind* films, Kirk is host of the Christian TV program *The Way of the Master.* (Dan Ewald, "The Rebirth of Kirk Cameron," *Today's Christian,* March/April, 2003; "Listen to Kirk's Testimony," The Way of the Master Web site.)

Did You Know? When Solomon wrote Ecclesiastes, he wrote it at the end of his life. He called himself *The Preacher,* which means "someone who gathers or assembles." Having seen the emptiness of fame, fortune, and power, Solomon wanted to shout his message loud and clear: *"Fear God, and keep His commandments,"* because that's all that matters in life (Ecclesiastes 12:13).

Another tidbit of interest is that after Solomon's reign, the kingdom of Israel divided into two kingdoms: The Southern Kingdom was called Judah; it continued to have an heir of David on the throne. The Northern Kingdom consisted of the tribes that pulled out of the united kingdom and was called the Kingdom of Israel.

Today's Prayer: *Dear God, I want to know You and live for You. Nothing else in this life really matters.*

Journal Question: Have you made time for really getting to know God—not doing God stuff, but *knowing* God? Write about those experiences.

_____

_____

_____

_____

_____

_____

_____

_____

_____

_____

_____

_____

_____

DAY 73

Can I really love those who've done me wrong?

Today's Teen: Naaman's Servant
Today's Action Verse: 2 Kings 5:3
Storyline: 2 Kings 5:1–14

Namaan's Servant Speaks Today: *"God wants you to love those persons you would like to hate, especially those who have done you wrong. Your love may bring them into the kingdom."*

Digging Deeper: This Israelite girl was captured by the enemy while she was in her teens and forced to be a servant for Syria's highest-ranking general. This unnamed, unknown, seemingly insignificant servant girl had no reason to care about her master's condition. Why should she care about Naaman? After all, it was he who had taken her captive. It was he who had forced her into slavery.

Other young persons may have viewed Naaman as an enemy, but this servant girl saw him as a person with a need. She sympathized with Naaman's crippling leprosy and helped him to find the cure. Because of her unselfishness, Naaman found his cure and found faith in God.

What is it that empowered this girl to love the unlovable? Did she do it to gain favor? Did she do it because it might buy her freedom? Or would you think, as I do, that she did it because her faith in God compelled her to? She practiced the principle Jesus shared hundreds of years later when he encouraged us to love our enemies.

Love your enemies? Do you think, *That's impossible?* Seek their best interests? That sounds kind of unrealistic. But that's what God wants you to do. In fact, God may have put these people in your life for a purpose—so your testimony could point them to His love.

Just Like You: OK, it's easy to talk to your friends and family about Christ, but what about the loner with the trench coat or the loudmouth who mocks Christians? Sharing Christ with the unlovable can be difficult. Examining this servant girl's attitude, we can gain some pointers:

- **She wasn't bitter.** This Syrian captain and his army had taken away her future, forcing her to be a servant in a foreign culture. She had no title, no social standing, no money—nothing to make her excited about her life. Still she didn't allow bitterness to creep in, to color her attitude. She handled herself in such a respectful way that Naaman and his family were willing to listen to her advice.
- **She wasn't intimidated by Naaman's power.** She had something Naaman needed. It didn't matter that they were worlds apart. She knew who had the cure for his leprosy. She didn't allow fear to keep her from sharing the life-changing message.
- **She gained trust.** Why would an important person like Naaman listen to his servant girl? Because she evidently had gained his trust by hard work, a good attitude, and sympathy for him in his condition. So when the time came to share about what her God could do, Naaman was all ears.

Did You Know? Leprosy is a disease that affects the nervous system and keeps the body from feeling pain. In the Bible, lepers were outcasts and often forced to live in special areas, set apart from the rest of society. They were considered unclean.

Today's Prayer: *God, it's hard to love and forgive those people who have wronged me. Everything inside of me wants to seek their destruction. But I know I'm called to love them as You love me. Help me do it.*

Journal Question: Do you have trouble forgiving people? How can you possibly find the strength to love people who hurt you? If you have managed to forgive persons who did you wrong, describe how it made you feel.

_____

_____

_____

_____

_____

_____

Can I trust God to keep His promises?

Today's Teen: Joash
Today's Action Verse: 2 Chronicles 13:5
Storyline: 2 Chronicles 22:11–12

Joash Speaks Today: *"God's promises to believers are unbending, and you can claim them as your own."*

Digging Deeper: Joash was born during a bloody revolution and chaos in Judah, and the sparing of his life is vivid proof that God fulfills His promises to His people.

Hundreds of years earlier, God promised that a Messiah would come through King David's family line, but the wicked Queen Athaliah, Joash's grandmother, tried to put a stop to that line. She wanted to get rid of all the remaining heirs to her dead husband's throne, the royal descendants, so she killed all of her grandsons, or so she thought. But God raised up a godly aunt, Jehoshabeath (a.k.a. Jehosheba), who hid Joash in a private room. For six years, Joash, hidden in the house of God, was with his aunt and uncle, the priest. There, he was fed and taught the ways of the Lord. Through this secretive upbringing, Joash, the remaining descendant of David's throne, lived to continue the line of kings.

Again, Joash's life is proof that God keeps His promises. Even the most trusted people break their word or promises, but God never does. He'll never let you down.

He promised that Abraham would be the father of many nations, and it happened. He promised Moses that he would be used to deliver the children of Israel, and it happened. He promised David that out of his family line the Messiah would be born, and it happened with the birth of Jesus. He promised a Messiah who would pay for the sins of the world, and *it happened!*

If you've been disappointed by people you thought you could trust, don't let that bother you. They are just people. But you can cling to God's promises because He is God and He keeps His promises.

Just Like You: Did you know that God has made many promises that are for every believer? At least 40 promises have been counted. Here are a few:

- Everlasting life   John 3:16
- Assurance of salvation   1 John 5:13; John 10:28
- A heavenly home   John 14:1–3
- Answers to prayer   1 John 5:14–15
- Abundant life   John 10:10
- Forgiveness of sins   1 John 1:9
- Comfort   John 14:16, 18
- Friendship   John 15:15
- Gifts of the Spirit   1 Corinthians 12
- Freedom   Romans 8:2; John 8:32, 36
- Growth   Ephesians 4:11–15
- God's enabling power   John 14:12; Acts 1:8
- Victory over sin and death   1 John 5:4
- Peace   John 14:27
- Hope   Hebrews 6:18–19
- Wisdom   James 1:5
- A heavenly inheritance   1 Peter 1:3–4

Did You Know? At the age of seven, Joash was anointed king in a special ceremony arranged quickly by Jehoiada, a priest in Judah who was married to Jehoshabeath, Joash's aunt. With five military officers present, Jehoiada anointed this young boy as king to prevent Athaliah, Joash's grandmother, from continuing her wicked and cruel reign.

Today's Prayer: *Dear God, thank You for giving me Your precious promises. I know that I can claim each one as my own and that each one is a like an unbreakable contract between You—the all-mighty, all-powerful, perfect God—and myself.*

Journal Question: What promises of God will you claim?

_____

_____

_____

_____

_____

_____

_____

_____

_____

_____

_____

_____

_____

_____

_____

_____

_____

_____

Am I coasting on my parents' Christianity?

Today's Teen: Joash
Today's Action Verse: 2 Chronicles 24:17
Storyline: 2 Chronicles 24:17–20

Joash Speaks Today: *"Don't try to coast on the faith of the persons who raised you, but make your own choice to follow God."*

Digging Deeper: Joash was a bright light in a dark time in the history of Judah; he was miraculously preserved to lead Judah out of spiritual decay and back toward God. He was anointed king at the age of seven and followed God most of his early life. Lacking parents, he was raised in a godly home by his uncle, Jehoiada, and his aunt, Jehosheba.

But Joash had a problem. He lacked the deep roots in the faith that his uncle had, and so his faith withered when it was tested. While his uncle, Jehoiada, was alive and giving Joash good counsel, Joash followed God. But when his uncle died, Joash lost his spiritual edge. He turned away from God and began serving idols. He even killed one of Jehoiada's sons, a prophet from God, who came to warn Joash.

Joash evidently never made his uncle's faith his own. He lived off his spiritual heritage instead of making his own spiritual choices.

So what happens when your parents, your youth pastor, or your teachers are gone? What happens when you're forced to defend your faith or to demonstrate what you believe? This is where the rubber meets the road. This is where your true faith is revealed.

Don't make Joash's mistakes. Don't try to coast through life on your parents' Christianity. Determine what you believe and why.

Just Like You: "How do you really know that there's a God? Do you ever think sometimes that this stuff is just made up?"

The words of a co-worker struck fear into the heart of Kylie as she cleaned out her drawer and prepared to go home after finishing a night shift at her new job.

Kylie was afraid because she believed God was true, but she'd always go to her dad for answers. But here she was, being confronted with a real serious question, and she couldn't provide an answer. She'd sat in church her whole life, but she never really absorbed the preaching. She'd always obeyed her parents and pastor and was on her way to Bible College. So why couldn't she answer a question that addressed the core of her faith?

"Umm, look, I've really got to go now, so can we talk about this more another day?" Kylie said.

"You don't have an answer, do you? Do you?" smirked her co-worker.

"Ahh, I have to go!" Kylie said as she rushed out of the grocery store and ran to her car. Tears rolled down her face. "God, I've grown up in church, I've gone to a Christian school, and I can't answer the most basic question about my faith!"

Right now, as a youth, spend time with God in His Word. Let Him become real to you. Dig out answers to hard questions. Dig down to the rock and build your faith on it.

Did You Know? Joash had to survive Queen Athaliah's wicked genocide because he was the last surviving descendant of David's royal line, and God had promised Israel that the Messiah would come from David's family.

Today's Prayer: *Help me to look at the life of Joash and learn from his mistakes. I want to glean wisdom from the godly influences in my life, but I also want to let Your Word soak deeply into my heart and soul so that my faith will be strong in the storms of life. I want my faith to be my own.*

Journal Question: Do you believe what you believe just because your mom or dad believes it? Or have you taken ownership of God's Word, and let it soak deep into your heart? How has God's Word changed what you believe?

_____

_____

_____

_____

_____

_____

_____

_____

_____

✣ ✣ ✣ ✣ ✣ ✣ ✣ ✣ ✣ ✣   ✣ ✣ ✣ ✣ ✣ ✣ ✣ ✣ ✣

How can I make a difference for Christ?

Today's Teen: Josiah
Today's Action Verses: 2 Kings 22:2; 2 Chronicles 34:3
Storyline: 2 Kings 22:1 through 23:30; 2 Chronicles 34:3–7

Josiah Speaks Today: *"You can make a difference. You can stand up for God in your church, school, and community."*

✣ ✣

Digging Deeper: God had extended mercy toward His people for many generations, and they repaid the Lord by following after other gods and engaging in all kinds of wickedness. So God was ready to lift His hand of protection and allow the other nations to judge Judah. But then came along a young man who decided to stand up in the midst of the wickedness and lead Judah out of spiritual darkness. His name was Josiah, and he became king at the tender age of eight.

It wasn't until he was 16 that Josiah began to really get serious about God. Even though growing up with a wicked father and a wicked grandfather, Josiah was able to reverse the course for his life; he decided to follow God. Something about God must have pricked deep in Josiah's heart, and under his watch, he led Judah to worship only the one true God. Josiah demonstrated leadership in a culture that hated God.

Maybe you can do the same thing in your school, church, or home. Maybe your parents don't live for God—but that doesn't mean you can't take a stand for Him. Maybe your friends think that smoking is no big deal and that getting drunk, taking drugs, and having sex outside of marriage are OK, but that doesn't mean you have to go along.

Josiah knew what it meant to be a teen leader. Maybe God is calling you do the same.

Just Like You: In May 2006, Brittany McComb, an honor student and valedictorian of her class at Foothill High School in Henderson, Nevada, submitted a rough draft of her graduation speech to school officials. A few days later Brittany received her rough draft back full of edits. Mostly, they had crossed out her references to God and Jesus Christ. They said that Brittany would be "proselytizing" and "pushing her religion on other students" if she gave her speech as written. They warned her not to give the speech as she had originally prepared it.

Over the next few weeks, Brittany had a decision to make. She could give the sanitized speech and, thus, gut the entire foundation of her testimony (the power of Jesus Christ working through her life), or she could deliver the speech and risk punishment.

When graduation day arrived, Brittany made her decision. When she got up to the podium, she started delivering her original speech. When she shared about Jesus Christ, her microphone was cut off by school administrators who feared a lawsuit by the ACLU. But the crowd sided with Brittany. They jeered when the microphone was turned off. Brittany became an instant celebrity and was able to share her testimony on *The Today Show, Fox News,* and other media outlets. So Brittany may have lost her right to free speech in one arena, but that event opened new opportunities to share her faith.

Did You Know? Josiah's great-grandfather was Hezekiah, who had been Judah's last godly king. Hezekiah's son and grandson—Josiah's grandfather and father—turned away from God and led Judah down a wicked path of idolatry and sin.

Today's Prayer: *Dear God, please give me the boldness and courage to stand up for You and lead others to honor You in today's wicked world.*

Journal Question: In what situations have you been tempted to go along with the crowd even when you knew it was wrong? What did you do? Why? On the other hand, how have you led others to do what is right in God's sight?

_____

_____

_____

_____

_____

_____

_____

_____

_____

_____

_____

_____

_____

_____

_____

_____

_____

_____

_____

✛ ✛ ✛ ✛ ✛ ✛ ✛ ✛ ✛ ✛   ✛ ✛ ✛ ✛ ✛ ✛ ✛ ✛ ✛ ✛ ✛

Do I have to repeat the sins of my parents?

Today's Teen: Josiah
Today's Action Verse: 2 Chronicles 34:2
Storyline: 2 Chronicles 33:21–25

Josiah Speaks Today: *"You don't have to continue the sins of your parents. You can reverse the trend and a make a difference with your life."*

✛ ✛

Digging Deeper: Josiah was not raised in a godly home. He was not taught by his father or grandfather to serve the Lord. Contrarily, he grew up under a father and grandfather who did evil in the sight of the Lord. And the culture in Judah was soaked with immoral sex and pagan worship.

In spite of all that stuff that would normally lead a person away from the Lord, Josiah followed God. He didn't allow the "sins of his fathers" to pass down to his life. He reversed that dangerous trend. How? When he was 16, he made a bold choice to seek after God and obey Him.

This example should put to rest the false idea that you're bound by the sins of your parents. Some persons teach that God won't bless you until you confess every sin your mother and father committed. But this is not true. Each generation makes its own choices and is held responsible only for the choices it makes.

No matter where you've come from, God wants you to start seeking after Him now, right where you are, and He can make you into a leader like Josiah.

Just Like You: If Rod fears anything, it's that he will slip into the same patterns of his father and his grandfather. Stretching back several generations, the men in his family have struggled with alcoholism. Rod has seen its devastation rip through homes like a tornado, leaving only destruction in its wake.

Sadly, Rod continues to hear that he is bound to continue this unfortunate family legacy. Even some Christian counselors tell him he has to "purge himself of the sins of his fathers" before he can get victory. The problem with Rod is that he doesn't even know all the sins his family members have committed! The burden on Rod is so great.

But when Rod became a Christian, he had newfound confidence. He realized that by not using alcohol, he could avoid the mistakes of his father. But better yet, with the power of the Holy Spirit inside of him, Rod could begin to establish a new tradition in his family, one of solid spiritual leadership. Young men like Josiah, who reversed the family curse of sin and idolatry, are encouragements to him.

Armed with God's power, inspired by his biblical heroes, and unfazed by the doubters, Rod is now determined to be a leader in his family.

Did You Know? Before Josiah's reforms began, the people of Judah were participating in evil pagan rituals. One place, named Tophet, was a shrine where babies were sacrificed and their ashes were offered up to false gods.

Today's Prayer: *Dear God, please give me strength to stand up and be my own person, in spite of any mistakes and failings of my parents.*

Journal Question: How can you escape the sins that may have plagued your parents? How can you be set free?

_____

_____

_____

_____

_____

_____

Is Bible reading that important?

Today's Teen: Josiah

Today's Action Verse: 2 Chronicles 34:21

Storyline: 2 Chronicles 34:14–21

Josiah Speaks Today: *"Bible reading is important. If you ignore it, you cut yourself off from God's source of power and wisdom."*

Digging Deeper: Do you ever go down to your basement or up to your attic and look through a box of books? They get quite dusty after sitting there for several years. Well, imagine how dusty the Old Testament Scriptures were when Josiah's priest found them. They had been hidden and preserved in a secret part of the Temple. When the Scriptures were read aloud, Josiah realized that God's people in Judah and Israel were not living according to His instructions, and so Josiah became distressed. He made several changes right away.

The Bible is an amazingly accurate mirror. It reveals the way you really are, not the way you think you are. It shows you where you are wrong and where you need to change. That's why the devil is often so intent on getting people to stop reading God's Word. The devil doesn't want anyone to grow, to change, and to experience God's best; he prefers everyone stay in his or her mediocre, immature condition.

Bible reading is so important to your daily growth. Even if it's just a chapter or even just a verse a day, it's important. Why? Because you need the daily cleansing that the Word provides (John 15:3). God's Word is a mirror that shows your imperfections and how God can help you change.

Just Like You: Get the most from your Bible readings. Here are some fresh tips for making your time with God come alive:

- **Focus on quality rather than quantity.** If you are feeling like you have to read six chapters a day to be spiritual and experiencing guilt if you don't, think again. It's better to read six verses, or even just one verse, and meditate on it. Absorb it. Digest it. Let it change the way you think and live.

- **Do a word study.** If you have access to Bible software, do a search on a word in the Bible—possibly love, forgiveness, or hope to start. Meditate on some of these verses and what they mean to you.

- **Use devotional helps (like this book!).** Sometimes it's good to have a devotional book to help guide you and explain what the Scripture is talking about. Remember, though, that the words of man are different from the Word of God. The words of man are good and helpful, but should not be your main source. The Word of God is the unchanging truth and should always be your main source.

- **Use a study Bible.** Two popular study Bibles for teens are the *Student's Life Application Bible* and the *Extreme Teen Bible*. Other good study Bibles include *The Daily Walk Bible* and the *Ryrie Study Bible*. Filled with charts, helpful background information, and character profiles, these Bibles can help you dig deeper into God's Word.

- **Memorize Scripture.** Each day, select one verse, and memorize it. Post it on a sticky note in your school folder, on your locker, or above your mirror. You'll be surprised how quickly these verses, once memorized, come to mind when you're going through a tough time.

Did You Know? Josiah reigned during one of the most important periods in world history. It was during his reign that the Assyrians were defeated and the Babylonian Empire rose to power.

Today's Prayer: *Dear Lord, thank You for giving me the rich gift of Your holy and inspired Word. Help me to be diligent and study it so I can gain wisdom in all areas of my life.*

Journal Question: Do you find it hard to read the Bible every day? What could you do differently that would motivate you to seek God in His Word daily? Who could hold you accountable; who could be your accountability partner?

_____

_____

_____

_____

_____

_____

_____

_____

_____

✛ ✛ ✛ ✛ ✛ ✛ ✛ ✛ ✛ ✛ ✛ ✛ ✛ ✛ ✛ ✛

What drastic steps do I have to take to remove sin from my life?

Today's Teen: Josiah
Today's Action Verse: 2 Chronicles 34:3
Storyline: 2 Chronicles 34:3–7

Josiah Speaks Today: *"If you want real change in your life, you have to take dramatic steps."*

✛ ✛ ✛ ✛ ✛ ✛ ✛ ✛ ✛ ✛ ✛ ✛ ✛ ✛ ✛ ✛ ✛ ✛ ✛ ✛

Digging Deeper: Josiah was interested in bringing about real change in the land under his charge, not cosmetic cover-ups. He was serious about getting people back into a right relationship with God. So what did he do?

He took drastic measures, tearing down all the idols and pagan temples and reestablishing true worship to God. His reforms probably created a lot of enemies, but Josiah knew he had to be serious about sin.

Victory over sin requires bold steps and real changes.

What "idols" are keeping you from the Savior? What influences are dragging you down? If you've got a secret sin, a habit you can't seem to break, take drastic measures. Get serious about rooting it out. If you really want victory, you have to get rid of the sin and then go a step further: embrace true worship of God. That means spending time alone with God. It means opening your Bible and digging into the Word. It means praying to the Savior. It means faithfully attending church and participating in group worship.

Victory over sin comes only when you get your heart and mind serious about the battle.

Just Like You: Emily loved Tuesday nights because Tuesday was the one night of the week that she didn't have to be anywhere or do anything. So, to relax, she usually sat on the couch and flipped through the television stations. The last several weeks, the girls at school had been talking about a new sitcom, so Emily started watching it. The first few weeks of the show were pretty funny, and the content was clean. But one week, the writers broke the ice. The plot revolved around some subjects that Emily knew were not appropriate, yet she continued to watch, silently justifying her action: *It's OK this once. I can handle it.*

The next week, the show got a little more risqué, and Emily grew a little more uncomfortable watching it. But she kept watching. A week later, Emily flipped on her newly favorite show. Sure enough, the writers pushed the envelope with images and subjects completely against her values. As Emily watched, her conscience protested louder and louder. When the closing credits finally scrolled down the screen, Emily cried. *I can't believe I just watched that. How could I have done that?*

Ashamed, Emily got on her knees and asked the Lord's forgiveness. Then she made a pact with God to reclaim Tuesday nights for Him. Not only would she turn off the TV, but she would do something more constructive, like call a friend, read a book, or write a letter. What's more, she would ask her mom and dad to keep her accountable regarding the promise she made to God.

Did You Know? The prophet Jeremiah wept (lamented) publicly when Josiah died (2 Chronicles 35:25). He must have known that Josiah's righteous leadership would be missed and that Judah would likely revert back to its sinful ways once its great king died.

Today's Prayer: *Dear Lord, reveal any secret sins in me. Please give me the strength to set things right and to resist future temptations. I don't want any hindrances to my walk with You.*

Journal Question: What sins are keeping you from God's purpose for your life? What dramatic steps do you need to take to eliminate the roots of such temptations?

_____

_____

_____

_____

_____

_____

_____

_____

_____

_____

_____

_____

_____

_____

_____

_____

Why can't I just have a comfortable Christian life?

Today's Teen: Jeremiah
Today's Action Verses: Jeremiah 1:4–5
Storyline: Jeremiah 1

Jeremiah Speaks Today: *"God called me away from my comfort zone into a radical life of service, sacrifice, and blessing."*

Digging Deeper: Jeremiah grew up in the Temple. His father was a respected priest and spiritual advisor to Josiah, the godly king who tried to lead the kingdom of Judah back to the Lord. Jeremiah may have thought he'd continue working as a priest in the Temple—a pretty comfy and straightforward job with no risks, no hardships, and no enemies.

But the word of the Lord came to Jeremiah with an announcement of his calling. Jeremiah was not called to be a *priest*; rather, the Lord had ordained him to be a *prophet.* In fact, before Jeremiah was even born, God had plans for this young man's life: Jeremiah would be a prophet standing alone and preaching God's words to a nation and a culture that just didn't want to hear. In other words, Jeremiah was called to move out of his comfort zone.

A lot of Christians want life to be easy. They like church, Christian music, and their good friends and don't care to step out of that world. But God doesn't necessarily want Christians to be comfortable. In fact, God has been known to allow Christians to be uncomfortable. In times like that, they are forced to rely on the power of the Holy Spirit.

Our culture is not so different from the one Jeremiah faced. God is calling young people like you to rock the boat and leave their comfort zone—calling them to make a difference.

Just Like You: Clay was halfway through his junior year and studying hard for the SAT exam. After talking with his parents and his guidance counselor at school, he was fairly sure he wanted to go to a local college to get an engineering degree. Engineers seemed to run in Clay's family, and he was promised an internship at his dad's company, a huge manufacturer that designed military equipment for the government.

Then one Sunday night, Clay's church showed the movie *End of the Spear,* the powerful story of Jim Elliot and the four other missionaries who were killed for bringing the Gospel to a native tribe in Ecuador. Afterward, a missionary from Ecuador stood up and spoke about the need for young people to come and help him in planting churches and building schools. He said they didn't need pastors, just young people who were good with their hands and could help with practical things, such as running phone and Internet lines. Moved by the powerful film and stirred to sacrifice by the example of Jim Elliot, Clay suddenly felt God calling him to this kind of missions work.

When Clay went home, he tried to talk himself out of it. But every day for a week, the Holy Spirit continued to speak to his heart. Finally, he told his parents about his struggle and wondered if he should at least take a short-term missions trip to Ecuador to see firsthand what needed to be done.

Clay's parents agreed and didn't try to talk him out of it, which was a surprise to Clay. He went back to his room, thinking, *God may want me to go to college someday, but right now I know He wants me in Ecuador.*

Did You Know? In Jeremiah's day and land, Judah, there was a huge difference between a priest and a prophet. A priest fulfilled ceremonial duties, which were mostly scripted out for him. A prophet, however, answered directly to God and was responsible for carrying God's message, which was often unpopular, to the people. Prophets would sometimes predict the future; they also would share God's pleasure or displeasure with His people.

Today's Prayer: *Dear God, a part of me wants life to be easy and comfortable, but I know You have bigger plans for me. Please help me to be flexible and willing to go where You want me to go.*

Journal Question: Why might God allow your life to be uncomfortable? What are some uncomfortable things God might want you to endure?

_____

_____

_____

_____

_____

✠ ✝ ✠ ✝ ✠ ✝ ✠ ✝ ✠ ✝ ✠ ✝ ✠ ✝ ✝ ✠ ✝ ✠ ✝ ✠ ✝ ✠ ✝ ✠ ✝

Am I important to God, or am I just another random person?

Today's Teen: Jeremiah
Today's Action Verse: Jeremiah 1:5
Storyline: Jeremiah 1

Jeremiah Speaks Today: _"You are not on this earth by chance. Before you were even born, God designed a plan for your life, and He wants to see it fulfilled in you."_

✠ ✝ ✠ ✝ ✠ ✝ ✠ ✝ ✠ ✝ ✝ ✠ ✝ ✠ ✝ ✠ ✝ ✠ ✝ ✝ ✠ ✝ ✠ ✝ ✠ ✝ ✠ ✝

Digging Deeper: Have you ever felt unimportant? Have you ever felt as if you really didn't matter to the people around you? Maybe you feel like no more than a statistic or a number. Maybe you feel kind of insignificant.

Jeremiah's calling should give you hope that you are special to God. God's words to Jeremiah echo today. Before Jeremiah was even born, God had a special purpose and plan for this young man's life. He was born in a certain place and at a specific time to make an impact on his world.

And so it is with you. There are no accidents with God. Your parents, your siblings, your gifts, your body, your friends—all these work together to accomplish His purpose in your life. He wants you, in your own unique way, to make a difference in this world.

Evolution teaches that we all kind of randomly evolved and are here without any real purpose. But God's Word gives you promise, hope, and direction. Before the foundations of the world were formed, God knew you would be who you are.

You are no accident, no freak of nature, no random person just floating out there without purpose. You live in this time and place because God wanted it that way.

Just Like You: Herb Bolden nervously negotiated his way through the dark and dangerous passageways of the Louisiana Superdome—the smells of raw sewage, decaying bodies, and mold filling the air. He was one of 20,000 Hurricane Katrina refugees packed into this sports facility. He'd brought his mother and siblings here to seek refuge, asking God to spare their lives and bring them to safety. But as night after night passed in the Superdome, Herb wondered if God even heard his cry. *Am I important to God, or am I just another face in the crowd? Does He care about my mother and my siblings? Does He know what we are going through? Does He care about us here in this squalor?*

After a week, relief finally came for Herb and his family. A friend of the family, Hy McEnery, the local representative for Child Evangelism Fellowship, arranged for the Bolden family to find more permanent housing in Iowa. There, a generous church took them in, fed them, and clothed them.

In August 2006, Herb enrolled in Dayspring Bible College. He'd made a promise to the Lord: "If You rescue me and my family, I will serve You the rest of my life."

Did You Know? Jeremiah's father was Hilkiah, the high priest who discovered the book of the Law in the Temple during the reign of Josiah, the king of Judah.

Today's Prayer: *Dear God, thank You for creating me as a unique person with a purpose.*

Journal Question: How do you know that you're not just a random statistic on this earth? What assurances has God given you in His Word?

_____

_____

_____

_____

_____

_____

✛ ✛ ✛ ✛ ✛ ✛ ✛ ✛ ✛  ✛ ✛ ✛ ✛ ✛ ✛ ✛ ✛ ✛

Is there anything God can't help me do?

Today's Teen: Jeremiah
Today's Action Verses: Jeremiah 1:8–10
Storyline: Jeremiah 1

Jeremiah Speaks Today: *"Your weakness is the gateway to God's divine power."*

✛ ✛ ✛ ✛ ✛ ✛ ✛ ✛ ✛ ✛ ✛ ✛ ✛ ✛ ✛ ✛ ✛ ✛ ✛ ✛

Digging Deeper: Have you ever reached a moment in which you threw your hands in the air and said, "I just can't do it"? That's how Jeremiah seemed to feel. He had probably thought he was going to be a priest in the Temple, like his father was, but God gave him a much more difficult job. God called Jeremiah to prophesy of God's coming judgment. These people he was called to prophesy to didn't care about God and didn't care about the consequences of their sins.

Jeremiah felt completely inadequate. But in a sense, this is exactly the attitude God wanted. See, young Jeremiah was about to understand that human weakness is the gateway to God's divine strength. In fact, it isn't God's practice to use Christians who are strong in and of themselves. God wants people who are broken, empty, and weak. The Apostle Paul said, *"When I am weak, then am I strong"* (2 Corinthians 12:10).

And here's the simple, yet profound truth that got Jeremiah up and going and into service: Where God calls, God equips.

In *Be Decisive,* Bible teacher Warren Wiersbe makes a very interesting point: "When God calls us, however, He isn't making a mistake; and for us to hesitate or refuse to obey is to act on the basis of unbelief and not faith."

Just Like You: Emma was overwhelmed. As the first person off of Coach Landis's bench, she was used to coming into the volleyball game and delivering a few of her knockout serves. But today Emma had a bigger test. Ginger, the starting setter and star of the team, was sick with the flu. So Coach Landis asked Emma not only to start the biggest tournament of the year but also to be the fill-in setter. Emma was OK at setting, but she was not Ginger. The entire team would be depending on her. She'd have to be the floor leader. The entire team would key off of her. Emma didn't want to let the team down.

During warm-ups, Emma sat down next to Coach Landis. "I don't think I can do this," Emma said.

Coach Landis put down her clipboard and leaned in toward Emma. She put her arm around her and said, "Emma, I've seen you play, I know you can do this. But it's OK if you feel overwhelmed. That sets you up perfectly for God to work through you."

"I just feel like I'm going to let the entire team down."

"I know you're feeling the pressure, but remember the words of the Lord to the Apostle Paul: *'My grace is sufficient for thee: for my strength is made perfect in weakness.'** And remember Paul's response: *'Most gladly therefore will I rather glory in my infirmities, that the power of Christ may rest upon* *me.'** What that means is that feeling weak and powerless is OK because that is just the moment that God can use you in the most powerful way."

"So it's OK to feel like this?"

"Sure as long as you remember that with the Lord's strength, you can do anything†—even lead your team in a very important tournament."

* 2 Corinthians 12:9; † Philippians 4:13

Did You Know?
Jeremiah's ministry began during the reign of Josiah, Judah's last good king. Josiah reformed Judah by reestablishing true worship and tearing down the altars for false gods, but these were only cosmetic changes. The people's hearts remained cold.

Today's Prayer:
Dear God, I know that Your power can sustain me when I feel too weak. Please give me Your power and wisdom.

Journal Question:
What tough assignment do you have this week? Have you asked God for His special strength?

_____

_____

_____

_____

_____

_____

_____

_____

_____

_____

_____

_____

DAY 83

Does God have an answer for my excuses?

Today's Teen: Jeremiah
Today's Action Verse: Jeremiah 1:7
Storyline: Jeremiah 1

Jeremiah Speaks Today: *"God has an answer for every one of your excuses."*

Digging Deeper: "I can't speak." "I'm too young." Petrified of being a prophet, Jeremiah was ready with reasons why he couldn't possibly be the guy God wanted. Pronouncing God's judgment and calling a nation back to God would be a difficult job, and Jeremiah was filled with fear at the prospect. But God had an answer for every excuse Jeremiah voiced and even some he didn't. His youth didn't matter because his authority came from God, not man. What about Jeremiah's speaking? God would put the words directly in his mouth. As for the audience, God flat out told Jeremiah, they would resist him. But in doing so, they wouldn't be rejecting Jeremiah; they'd be rejecting God himself.

Jeremiah wasn't the first young person to question God seriously. He wasn't the first to offer excuses, and he certainly wasn't the last!

Maybe you're thinking of excuses for not following God: *I'm too young. Nobody will listen to me. My friends will think I'm weird.* But God has an answer for every one of your concerns too.

Just Like You: Jeremiah offered excuses, and God gave him answers. When God called Jeremiah to a higher, radical life, living in dependence upon Him,

Jeremiah, like most Christians, came loaded with plenty of excuses. God answered Jeremiah, and He also answers you.

- **Excuse:** *I'm too young!* Jeremiah was young, probably between 17 and 20 years old, when God called him to be a prophet in Judah. Why would kings and religious leaders listen to him? Who would take him seriously?
  God's answer: *Don't say you're too young, because I'm sending you, and if I'm sending you, nobody can stand in your way* (Jeremiah 1:7–8, 19).
- **Excuse:** *I don't know what to say.* Jeremiah had no experience at being a prophet. What would he say? What if he said the wrong thing? He seemed paralyzed by fear, maybe fear of failure.
  God's Answer: *I will put the right words in your mouth* (Jeremiah 1:7, 9). A prophet spoke God's words, not his own.
- **Unspoken Excuse:** *They won't listen to me.* The message God gave Jeremiah to share was not a popular message. The people of Judah didn't want to hear about their sins and their need for God's forgiveness and grace.
  God's Answer: *Wherever you go, I will be there with you to deliver you* (Jeremiah 1:8, 18–19). It wouldn't be an easy road for Jeremiah, but he would always know that God was right there and that nothing that happened to him was out of God's will.

Did You Know? The name *Jeremiah* means "Jehovah will lift up," "elevated of the Lord," "whom Jehovah has appointed," and "exalted of God."

Today's Prayer: *Dear God, please give me the courage to follow You, no matter what the cost.*

Journal Question: What are some of your excuses for not following God completely? How can you overcome those excuses?

_____

_____

_____

_____

_____

Teen People of the Bible

DAY 84

What right does God have over my life?

Today's Teen: Jeremiah
Today's Action Verses: Jeremiah 1:4–5
Storyline: Jeremiah 1:1–10

Jeremiah Speaks Today: *"God, as the Creator, not only has the right to tell you what to do with your life, but He has the best plan for your success."*

Digging Deeper: Do you ever wonder, *What right does God have over my life?* Maybe you think this question, but have really been afraid to ask it. Well if you've ever thought this, you wouldn't be the first. When Jeremiah was a teenager, he could have had similar thoughts. And God addressed Jeremiah's wonderings with an irrefutable statement: *I'm the Creator; I made you.*

God, as the Creator, has the right to tell us what to do with our lives. In Ephesians 2:10, we see that service for Him was the very purpose of our creation. To Jeremiah, He said, "Before you were even born, as you were forming in your mother's womb, I planned your entire life. I brought you into being for a specific purpose."

Now, if God were evil and couldn't be trusted, this information would make life pretty miserable. But God isn't evil. He's good. His essence is love. His nature is righteousness. His heart is compassion.

God does have a right to your life, because He created you for His purpose and equips you to fulfill your destiny. And you can trust His purpose to be good.

Just Like You: Evangelist D. L. Moody, who founded Moody Bible Institute, said this:

> A great many people are afraid of the will of God, and yet I believe that one of the sweetest lessons we can learn in the school of Christ is the surrender of our wills to God, letting Him plan for us and rule our lives.... I cannot look a day into the future. I do not know what is going to happen tomorrow; in fact, I do not know what may happen before night; so that I cannot choose for myself as well as God can choose for me and it is much better to surrender my will to God's will.
> —D. L. Moody ✠

Did You Know? The prophecies given by God to Jeremiah were written down by Baruch, Jeremiah's personal secretary (Jeremiah 36:4).

Today's Prayer: *Dear God, I know You are the Creator and Author of my life. I realize that Your plan for me is better than my plan. I ask that Your will be done in me.*

Journal Question: What right does God have over your life? What do you need to surrender to God?

_____

_____

_____

_____

_____

_____

_____

_____

_____

_____

Is crying for wimps?

Today's Teen: Jeremiah
Today's Action Verses: Lamentations 1:1–2
Storyline: Lamentations 1–5

Jeremiah Speaks Today: *"Don't be ashamed if God puts a passion in your heart regarding the spiritual condition of others."*

Digging Deeper: People cry for a lot of different reasons. Some cry when they watch an inspiring movie. Others lose it after their team drops a tough game. Then there are those times when a person is going through a tough trial, like the death of a loved one or the loss of a good friend.

Crying is really not something to be ashamed of. Tears are a way of revealing deep emotions. Jeremiah shed a lot of tears. In fact, he was called the Weeping Prophet. But Jeremiah wasn't blubbering over something lame. His heart was broken by the condition of his country and countrymen. Year after year, he proclaimed God's coming judgments, and nobody listened. Jeremiah's sorrow sprang from a heart that yearned to see his people find fulfillment in God.

What is the cry of your heart? Does it bother you to see young people choosing a life apart from God? Are you burdened by millions of souls around the world who need to hear the life-saving message of the gospel? Are you troubled by a culture that seems bent on thumbing its nose at biblical values?

If Jeremiah's cry is the cry of your heart, then get ready for God to use you for His glory.

Just Like You: Nobody knew Michele like Tamra did—not her parents, not her teachers, not her brothers. Tamra and Michele had been inseparable since they first met in gym class in grade school. But Tamra noticed Michele hadn't been herself of late. Ever since they had begun their freshman year at the new school, Michele had become more withdrawn, and she was missing church and blowing off youth group too. Tamra's bubbly, energetic friend had gone into hibernation.

Tamra was worried. At first she didn't want to say anything, but something inside her told her she had to approach Michele and at least find out what was wrong. So one afternoon after school, Tamra called Michele. Michele answered, but in a very short voice. After the usual small talk, Tamra got right into it: "What's wrong? I've noticed that you've changed."

Michele didn't want to talk about it. She was rude; and then click—she hung up.

Tamra was devastated. This had never happened in all the years of their friendship. She cried and cried.

Did anyone know what was wrong? She called some mutual friends and inquired about Michele. That's when she found out more about what was going on with Michele. She was stunned.

Michele had met a guy on MySpace and was now chatting with him every day. She was starting to question her beliefs and had even talked about moving in with her boyfriend.

Tamra wondered how Michele could walk away from everything she held dear. Then she stumbled on God's promise to Jeremiah, the guy who wept at the sight of his people turning from God: *"Then shall ye call upon me, and ye shall go and pray unto me, and I will hearken unto you"* (Jeremiah 29:12). She began immediately to cry out to God for her friend Michele.

Did You Know? Jeremiah's ministry spanned the reigns of five kings in Judah: Josiah (640–609 B.C.), Jehoahaz (609 B.C.), Jehoiakim (609–597 B.C.), Jehoiachin (597 B.C.), and Zedekiah (597–587 B.C.).

Today's Prayer: *Dear God, give me a passion for the people You love and the motivation to do something to bring them into Your kingdom.*

Journal Question: Have you ever been moved to tears? What caused the tears? What is the passion of your heart now?

_____

_____

_____

_____

_____

_____

_____

_____

_____

✛ ✛ ✛ ✛ ✛ ✛ ✛ ✛ ✛   **DAY 86**   ✛ ✛ ✛ ✛ ✛ ✛ ✛ ✛ ✛

Can I decide ahead of time to obey God?

Today's Teen: Daniel
Today's Action Verse: Daniel 1:8
Storyline: Daniel 1

Daniel Speaks Today: *"Don't wait until the hour of temptation to set your value system. Arm yourself for the battle well in advance."*

✛ ✛

Digging Deeper: Because Judah rejected God, He allowed this wayward nation to be captured by Babylon and their cruel king, Nebuchadnezzar.

Certain well-favored, skillful, cunning, knowledgeable youth from Judah were chosen to stay in the king's palace and learn the ways of the Chaldeans. Daniel and three of his friends, Shadrach, Meshach, and Abednego, were some of the young men of Judah chosen to stand in Nebuchadnezzar's court. For three years, these young men were given a crash course in the history, culture, and lifestyle of Babylon. The goal seemed to be to brainwash them, strip them of their allegiance to God, and create a new generation of Babylonian leaders.

The king of Babylon didn't realize what he had gotten in Daniel and his friends. They were different from their peers. They realized that the kingdom to which they had been brought was in conflict with the kingdom of God, and they purposed to hold God's laws in their hearts.

Fast forward several thousand years. Today, you're a Christian stuck in a culture that hates God and encourages you to ditch your values and embrace the god of self-satisfaction. You know you're supposed to be different, but you look around and see most of your Christian friends giving in and going with the flow.

Daniel and his three friends stood tall because they set their value systems before the hour of temptation—and so can you. Don't wait until you're weakened by the power of the enemy. Purpose now to keep God's Word in your heart and live by it.

Just Like You: Carter was a little nervous about starting high school. Even though he was going to a Christian school, he'd heard about the struggles of being a teenager and the potential trouble he could get into with wrong friends and bad choices. He also knew that his parents were looking for him to start policing himself—not having to be told a million times to do what he knew he should do.

He knew he'd have more responsibility. He knew temptations would surround him. So the summer before Carter began his freshman year, he read several books for teens suggested by his youth pastor. He had already committed to following Jesus a few years earlier, but he knew that he needed to reaffirm his commitment if he was going to make it spiritually, especially through the tough high school years. At the end of the summer, Carter made a vow before God. Like Daniel, he purposed ahead of time that he would follow God throughout high school, even in the tough times, even when he began to doubt his faith. Carter asked the Holy Spirit for strength and guidance because he knew he couldn't walk the journey alone.

Did You Know? In *Daniel: God's Man in a Secular Society,* Donald Campbell describes some characteristics of Daniel that equipped him for service in the king's court: "The requirements for selection were high ([Daniel] 1:4), but Daniel, along with his three friends, met them. We learn that Daniel had no physical blemish and was pleasing in appearance. Mentally, he was intelligent, knowledgeable, and quick to learn. Socially, he was poised and able to live in the king's court without creating embarrassment for himself or others. Daniel was an unusual teen-ager, a fact that Ashpenaz was apparently quick to recognize."

Today's Prayer: *Dear God, before the temptations come, I want to purpose in my heart to serve You; that way, I will be prepared with the strength and courage I need to resist them.*

Journal Question: Have you committed, as did Daniel, to follow God, even before temptation strikes? How does this make a difference?

_____

_____

_____

_____

_____

_____

_____

_____

_____

_____

_____

_____

_____

DAY 87

Are small compromises such a big deal?

Today's Teen: Daniel
Today's Action Verse: Daniel 1:12
Storyline: Daniel 1:8–21

Daniel Speaks Today: *"Take notice of little sins, because they are a big deal."*

✛ ✛

Digging Deeper: Daniel and his three friends, Shadrach, Meshach, and Abednego, cooperated with their Babylonian masters and endured three years of intense instruction. Even though they were living in a heathen culture, they dedicated themselves to becoming the very best they could be for God. But it wasn't an easy road from the start. These four young men had been faced early on with a faith-compromising issue: deciding whether to eat the king's food.

So what was the big deal about the food? Did they make a mountain out of a molehill? This conflict was over more than the strange menu. The food they were being asked to eat, though considered choice food, would likely have been offered in sacrifice to idols and some of it may have been unclean according to the Jewish Law. Now wasn't that a sneaky way for the king to get these guys to abandon their faith and embrace the culture of their new home?

What a monumental test! If they kept quiet, they'd probably earn favor with the king. If they refused, it might mean certain death by a ruler who took pleasure in executing those with whom he didn't get along. Could they trust God to take care of them if they stood up to the king in order to do what they considered right in the eyes of God? Or would they find a convenient way to explain away a slight disobedience to God?

What little tests are you facing today? What temptations to compromise are being dangled in front of you? What questionable activities are you being coerced into joining?

The real question is this: Do you trust God enough to obey Him?

Just Like You: What is the difference between compromising and being judgmental?

For Daniel and his friends, eating the king's food was a big deal because it directly violated God's law. But sometimes, issues aren't that black and white. Here are some questions to ask when weighing tough decisions:

- **Would your pastor or your parents be OK with the activity you're considering?** If not, then chances are, God wouldn't be OK with it either. If what you're doing has to be hidden from spiritual people whom you trust, you may be compromising your values.
- **Does what you are doing go against what you've been taught and know to be right according to God's Word?** If so, then no matter how small your sin may seem to be, it's still a sin and still a compromise.
- **Is this an issue in your life, or are you digging into someone else's problems?** If it's someone else's problems, then you're probably being judgmental.

Did You Know? King Nebuchadnezzar was known for his cruelty. Historians say he took pleasure in executing his enemies, even loved ones or palace staff, by throwing them into a furnace and laughing as they burned to death.

Today's Prayer: *Dear God, please give me strength to resist sin, even seemingly small sins.*

Journal Question: What sins have you been treating lightly? How can you overcome these sins and do what is right in God's sight?

_____

_____

_____

_____

_____

_____

_____

_____

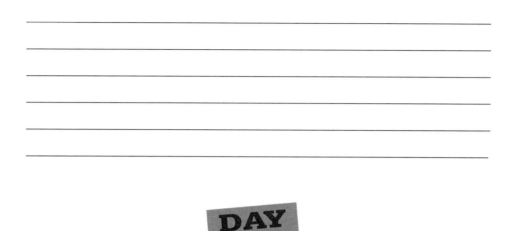

Will God take care of me if I obey Him?

Today's Teen: Daniel
Today's Action Verse: Daniel 1:12
Storyline: Daniel 1:8–21

Daniel Speaks Today: *"It wasn't really about the food, it was about my own heart. Would I follow God in the little things?"*

Digging Deeper: Before you adopt the radical Daniel diet, let's get to the heart of this story. It wasn't about the food. The food Daniel and his three friends ate had no more power to keep them healthy than anything else. A bowl of cereal and some vegetables contain no magic energy boost.

Instead, this test was about radical faith and obedience. These guys' held to their convictions through the test, trusting God with the results. Would

God take care of these guys as they obeyed Him, or would they end up worse than their peers?

It's the same question as those the young people ask today: *If I obey God, will He take care of me? If I listen to my spiritual authorities, will I be better off? If I save myself for marriage, will I really be happier? If I avoid the wrong crowd, will I ever have any friends?*

Daniel, Shadrach, Meshach, and Abednego faced a tough faith test. And God came through for them.

That same God will come through for you. Why not trust Him during your tests?

Just Like You: When Jay's parents both died in a car accident, he was given a choice by the state. He could live with a family from his church who offered to help him during his high school years or he could live with his uncle in California.

Either way, there were certain stipulations. If he stayed in his hometown, Jay would have to abide by the rules of his new family and be involved in their church. If he went to California, he would have to promise to "give up on the whole religious thing." His uncle offered to let him live in his sprawling mansion, complete with a pool, minigym, and recording studio. He'd not only have his own room, but he'd also have his own car.

So Jay was facing a test. With the church family, he'd have everything he needed spiritually. With his uncle, he'd have everything he needed materially.

After talking it over with his pastor, Jay decided on a trial. He'd live with the church family for a year. At the end of the year, if he wasn't happy, he could move. Jay's pastor told him, "Listen, if you follow God, He'll provide for your physical needs. But if you follow your own way, you may have your physical needs taken care of, but you'll never have peace, real inner peace. And peace is more valuable than any possession you can have."

Did You Know? What was this pulse that Daniel and his friends insisted on eating? Some think it was a vegetarian diet. Others say it was a form of cereal.

Today's Prayer: *Dear God, even though compromising my values makes life look easier, I trust that You will take care of me as I live in obedience to You.*

Journal Question: How do you know that God will take care of you? How has God taken care of you thus far in your life?

_____

_____

_____

_____

_____

_____

✜ ✛ ✜ ✛ ✜ ✛ ✜ ✛ ✜ ✛  ✜ ✛ ✜ ✛ ✜ ✛ ✜ ✛ ✜ ✜

How can I take a stand without being a jerk?

Today's Teen: Daniel
Today's Action Verse: Daniel 1:12
Storyline: Daniel 1:8–21

Daniel Speaks Today: *"God gave me the courage to take an unpopular stand, and He gave me the wisdom to be right without being a total jerk about it. God can do the same for you."*

✜ ✛ ✜ ✛ ✜ ✛ ✜ ✛ ✜ ✛ ✜ ✛ ✜ ✛ ✜ ✛ ✜ ✛ ✜ ✛ ✜ ✜

Digging Deeper: This popular story has another side. Did you notice the way Daniel stood up for his convictions? He didn't come across like an arrogant know-it-all. Daniel politely asked the person in authority over him to put his proposed plan to the test. Daniel was firm, but he wasn't a jerk. There is a difference.

Imagine what would have happened if Daniel had made a big stink about this issue. What if he'd pointed his finger in judgment at everyone else. What if Daniel had passed himself off as some kind of holier-than-thou guy. Not only would he have brought shame to his cause, but he might have been killed.

Jesus told His disciples to be *"wise as serpents, and harmless as doves"* (Matthew 10:16). Daniel was no angry Bible thumper, yet he stood his ground. Think of Joseph and David—how they handled very difficult situations with a mixture of courage, wisdom, and grace.

Think for a moment about the way in which you handle yourself, especially around those who don't see things the way you see them. Are you disagreeable? Are you judgmental? Are you preachy? You can hold firm to your convictions without alienating others. Your gentle spirit may mean the difference between someone listening to what you say and that person walking away.

Just Like You: How can I take a stand without acting like a jerk? We've all known those superspiritual people who are so good at telling everyone what to do; they sometimes come across as jerks. Daniel wasn't this kind of guy. He didn't get satisfaction by pointing out others' mistakes. Here are a few tips on standing up without sticking out like a sore thumb:

- **If possible, handle differences privately.** If you've got an issue with a friend or a person who is trying to get you to do something you know is wrong, talk it out with that person in private through a friendly conversation, email, or phone call. Don't embarrass him or her in front of everyone.
- **If you're with non-Christians, just politely say no.** Let's say you're at a family gathering and someone offers you alcohol to drink. Don't turn the dinner table into your own private soapbox. Just say, "No, thank you." If you lash out with Bible verses and sermons, you could turn people off toward Christianity.
- **Be humble.** Don't walk around with a chip on your shoulder as if you've got all the answers to life. Just because you made the right choice this time doesn't mean you'll always make the right choices. So demonstrate grace towards those who may have gotten it wrong.
- **Ask the Lord for wisdom.** Before you take a verbal stand, ask God for wisdom. Pray that the words you speak will be delivered with grace.

Did You Know? The Law of Moses restricted Israel from eating certain meats (Leviticus 11). These special laws have since been lifted and, thankfully, eating meat of any kind is no longer considered sinful (Acts 10:9–16).

Today's Prayer: *Dear God, please help me be bold in my witness and yet loving in my approach.*

Journal Question: Have you ever acted like a self-righteous jerk to your friends? What were the results? Has your prideful attitude ever turned away those who may be seeking the Savior? How can you change?

_____

_____

_____

_____

_____

_____

_____

_____

_____

_____

_____

_____

_____

_____

_____

_____

_____

DAY 90

Am I choosing friends who will affirm my beliefs?

Today's Teen: Daniel
Today's Action Verse: Daniel 1:12
Storyline: Daniel 1:8–21

Daniel Speaks Today: *"Choose friends who share your values."*

✛ ✛ ✛ ✛ ✛ ✛ ✛ ✛ ✛ ✛ ✛ ✛ ✛ ✛ ✛ ✛ ✛ ✛ ✛ ✛

Digging Deeper: Lots of times peer influence is given a bad rap, like if your friends want you to watch a bad movie, play a practical joke, or make fun of some helpless person. On your own, you may not feel comfortable doing those things, but with a group, it is easy to get drawn into a wrong activity.

Well, Daniel discovered that this same principle, peer influence, can be a positive thing. He chose to hang out with three other like-minded teenagers. Each of them was willing to stand up for their convictions on their own, but together they were even stronger. What a band of brothers these guys were! They were bound by a common passion for God.

When you have to do something tough, it can be easier if you have friends who stand with you. Proverbs says good friends are like iron sharpening iron (Proverbs 27:17). That is one reason why attending church is so important. God never intended for the Christian life to be lived in isolation. He intended for you to live out your faith in community with other like-minded believers.

Just Like You: Bobby, Jon, and Sherry are pretty tight. Because they are all homeschooled kids, they hang out at each other's house quite a bit when they're not working on a church project or volunteering at the local crisis pregnancy center.

When a rumor began spreading around town about their pastor, Bobby, Jon, and Sherry jointly sprang into action. They knew for a fact that the rumor wasn't true and that their pastor was a godly man, so they felt like they had to do something to stop the rumor.

Bobby, Jon, and Sherry first went to the pastor and made him aware of what was being said. They not only encouraged him but told him they were going to put a stop to what was being said. Then the three friends approached the person in the church who was responsible for the rumor and confronted him, gently, but firmly.

The man resisted at first, but was impressed by the resolve of these three determined teens. He backed down and agreed that he was wrong. Later that night, the teens received an email that had been sent to a bunch of other people with an apology from the talebearer. He said the courage of these teens convinced him to do the right thing.

Did You Know? We know Daniel's three friends as Shadrach, Meshach, and Abednego, but their real names—the Jewish names they were given at birth—were Hananiah, Mishael, and Azariah. When they were captured, they were given the Babylonian names by which we know them. Daniel, too, was given a Babylonian name, Belteshazzar.

Today's Prayer: *Dear Lord, surround me with friends who encourage me to stand up for my beliefs.*

Journal Question: How are your friends influencing your faith?

_____

_____

_____

_____

_____

_____

_____

DAY 91

Would I be willing to die for my faith?

Today's Teens: Shadrach, Meshach, Abednego
Today's Action Verses: Daniel 3:16–18
Storyline: Daniel 3:1–30

Shadrach, Meshach, and Abednego Speak Today:

"Sometimes you just have to stand up for your faith, even if you have to stand alone."

Digging Deeper: The first time Shadrach, Meshach, and Abednego were pressured to disobey God, their friend Daniel was the one who stood up to the king's officer and took the flak. All they had to do was follow his lead. But now they were on their own, and the stakes were much higher.

Nobody really knows where Daniel was at this time, but we do know that these three young men were willing to stand for their faith even without the leadership of their strong-faithed friend and even if it meant losing their lives.

Notice that they were the only three Jewish young people mentioned who refused to bow down to Nebuchadnezzar's golden image, just like they, along with Daniel, were the only ones reported to be intent on obeying the Jewish dietary laws while in captivity (Daniel 1). They were forced to choose first between their comfort and their faith, and later between their life and their faith. But with each passing test, standing strong became easier.

As for the many Jewish youth in Babylonian captivity who caved in to the pressure, compromising also became much easier the second, third, and fourth times.

How did Shadrach, Meshach, and Abednego resist the pressure to cave in? They made the decision long before the order to bow ever came. Before they even stepped foot in Babylon, they'd determined to live life God's way, even if it cost them popularity, money, or their lives. They'd died to themselves and, in doing so, were not afraid of the worst that man could do to them.

Just Like You: What do you do when you face a fiery furnace or pressure to compromise? When it comes to making a decision about something you know goes against what you believe, you have only three choices: go with the flow, run, or stand. Let's walk through the options Shadrach, Meshach, and Abednego may have had and compare them with the choices you often face:

1. **Go with the flow.** The reasons for giving in and playing nice with the pressure to compromise are endless. Here are a few:

   • *Don't I owe it?*

   Shadrach, Meshach, and Abednego had really good jobs that the king had given them. Didn't they owe it to him to play along?

   For you, the test might be a relationship with a boy or girl who is pressuring you to go further. You feel you owe him or her something and don't want to hurt that person. But at this point, who would you rather please? The person who is pressuring you or God? Are you really doing the other person a favor by giving in?

   • *Going along doesn't have to mean I agree. I can fake it.*

   Shadrach, Meshach, and Abednego might could have faked it by bowing down to the golden image, but not really meaning it. But what testimony would that have sent to the unbelieving people around them? Would it have indicated that their faith couldn't stand up to the heat?

   For you, the test might be peer pressure to view a questionable movie. You know it's wrong, but you don't want to lose your friends. However, if you do view it, they may no longer take your faith seriously.

   • *Even if I go along now, God will forgive me if I ask.*

   Shadrach, Meshach, and Abednego might could have bowed down to save their lives and then quickly asked God for forgiveness.

   Sure, God is quick to forgive our sins (1 John 1:9). But what does it say about your heart when you deliberately "game the system" by taking advantage of His grace? God's grace and forgiveness are complete, but that doesn't erase consequences.

2. **Run away.** Actually we're not sure whether Shadrach, Meshach, and Abednego could have run away, but many teens choose this option—escaping the heat of the temptation. This option might not be ideal, but it is better than giving in.

3. **Stand up for God.** This could have cost Shadrach, Meshach, and Abednego a lot: not just their cushy jobs with lots of money and perks, but their very lives. By standing for God, they proved that faith in God is fireproof, and that He is more powerful than the most powerful king.

What message can you convey by standing for God? You never know who may be watching you. Maybe someone in your school, neighborhood, or church is searching for the truth. Will they see it lived out in you?

Did You Know? Furnaces in Babylon were a lot bigger than your average house furnace. They were very large and used for firing bricks and for the ironsmith's forge. Fueled by charcoal, they could produce incredibly high temperatures. A typical furnace was made up of a series of tunnels with several large entrances, which served as ventilation shafts. It is likely the three guys were thrown into one of those.

Today's Prayer: *Dear God, give me the courage to stand for You, especially when I know I will take flak for it. Help me to carry myself wisely.*

Journal Question: Are you willing to take a stand, and willing to do it wisely and lovingly? Why or why not?

_____

_____

_____

_____

_____

_____

_____

DAY 92

Why does God allow Christians to be persecuted?

Today's Teens: Shadrach, Meshach, Abednego
Today's Action Verse: Daniel 3:28
Storyline: Daniel 3

These Three Guys Speak Today: *"Suffering for our faith can be a privilege that allows us to point others to a relationship with God."*

Digging Deeper: Why would God allow Shadrach, Meshach, and Abednego to go through this fiery trial? (Pardon the pun.) Hadn't they endured enough, being ripped from their homes, taken to a strange country, and made to serve a ruthless dictator like Nebuchadnezzar? Now they were faced with a choice of bowing before a false god or perishing in the flames of a furnace.

At the end of this story, we see evidence that God's divine purpose was to show His glory to a society that had rejected Him and to bring His power to a people who had never known His name. The willingness of these young men to yield their lives to the will of God caused untold numbers of people to cast off their worship of idols and embrace the truth.

And so it is with the trials you face. You may not see the end of your story until you get to heaven. You may not fully understand the purpose of your fiery furnace. But you can be sure that God's purpose in your suffering is just as real as it was for those three guys in Babylon. God wants to use your life as a beacon of hope to those who don't yet know Him.

Teen People of the Bible

That's one reason it's important to stay strong in your faith. Your trials are much bigger than you. Your fiery furnace is your stage. Your enemy is God's divine tool in sharing the message. Your suffering allows you to be a part of God's redemptive plan.

Just Like You: When Holly became a Christian at the age of 17, her Jewish parents were upset with her. They thought she'd betrayed their faith, and they tried to keep her from going to church. But Holly knew she had to stand up for Christ, even if it meant moving out and getting an apartment. Her parents finally relented, but the persecution didn't stop.

When Holly married Mike, a leader in her church, her parents grew cold and distant. They attended the wedding, but they kept their distance. Every conversation seemed to include subtle shots at the Christian faith. Her parents called her extreme, obsessed, and crazy. Hearing them talk like that was hard on Holly. At times, she wished the conflict and unpleasant remarks would go away, but she always felt the Lord encouraging her to firmly and gently hold her ground.

Gradually over the next 20 years, Holly's parents grew to tolerate her Christian faith, but never fully accepted it. Then, at a funeral for a mutual friend, Holly's mother heard the gospel message, and at that time and at that place, it made sense to her. The next day Holly got a call.

"You'll never believe this," her mom said, "but I've become a Christian."

Holly wept.

"I heard the message yesterday," her mom continued, "but the greatest testimony to me was your faith through all the persecution I gave you. Thank you for standing strong."

A few years later, Holly's mother was diagnosed with cancer and passed away. But Holly had complete peace, knowing that the trial she had endured all those years had a purpose: the salvation of her mother.

Did You Know? Nebuchadnezzar's dedication ceremony for the golden image he made was a festive event, with dignitaries, musicians, and artists gathered on the plain of Dura. A great multitude of people of different nations and languages came together for the event.

Today's Prayer: *Dear God, thank You for the privilege of suffering for You. Help my life reflect Your love for those who don't know You.*

Journal Question: What trials are you currently suffering, and how does your attitude in the trials reflect God's love to unbelievers?

_____

_____

_____

_____

_____

_____

✢ ✣ ✢ ✢ ✢ ✢ ✢ ✢ ✢ ✣  ✢ ✣ ✢ ✢ ✢ ✢ ✢ ✢ ✣

Does God know what other people are doing to me?

Today's Teens: Shadrach, Meshach, Abednego
Today's Action Verse: Daniel 3:25
Storyline: Daniel 3

These Three Guys Speak Today: _"With every trial you face, you can face it, not in your own strength alone, but with all the power of heaven and earth."_

✢ ✣ ✢ ✢ ✢ ✢ ✢ ✢ ✣ ✢ ✢ ✢ ✢ ✢ ✣ ✢ ✢ ✢ ✢ ✢ ✢ ✢ ✣ ✢

Digging Deeper: Imagine how alone Shadrach, Meshach, and Abednego must have felt as they defied the world's most powerful king. A multitude of people, including their Jewish brethren in that land, must have been very interested in seeing what the king would do about it.

Now imagine how encouraged those three guys must have felt when that fourth Someone, whom Nebuchadnezzar said was *"like the Son of God"* (Daniel 3:25), showed up to walk with them through their fiery punishment.

You might say, "I could easily resist temptation if I knew that God was going to be with me." But you *do* have that assurance. That's right. God is with you. You have the Holy Spirit living inside of you. Jesus promised the disciples that when He went back to the Father, after His death, resurrection, and ascension, the Holy Spirit would come (John 16:7; Acts 1:8). If you have received Jesus Christ as your Lord and Savior, the Holy Spirit lives inside of you and empowers you with all the resources of God Himself.

So when you face trials and temptations, you have the same power that defeated sin and death when Jesus rose from the grave. That power is available to you in the Holy Spirit. The Holy Spirit helps you to fight your battles, endure your fiery furnaces, and reflect God's love to an unbelieving world.

Just Like You: In the classic devotional and journal *Experiencing God Day-by-Day,* the following is said about the work of Christ in the believer:

> The heavenly Father's plan from the beginning of time was to place His eternal Son in every believer. If you are a Christian, all the fullness of God dwells in you. Christ's life becomes your life. When Christ lives in you, He brings every divine resource with Him. Every time you face a need, you meet it with the presence of the crucified, risen, and triumphant Lord of the universe inhabiting you. When God invites you to become involved in His work, He has already placed His Son in you so that He can carry out His assignment through your life.
>
> This has significant implications for your Christian life. Discipleship is more than acquiring head knowledge and memorizing Scripture verses. It is learning to give Jesus Christ total access to your life so He will live His life through you. Your greatest difficulty will be believing that your relationship with Christ is at the heart of your Christian life. When others watch you face a crisis, do they see the risen Lord responding? Does your family see the difference Christ makes when you face a need? What difference does the presence of Jesus Christ make in your life?

God wants to reveal Himself to those around you by working mightily through you. He wants your family to see Christ in you each day. God wants to express His love through your life. There is a great difference between "living the Christian life" and allowing Christ to live His life through you.

—Henry T. Blackaby and Richard Blackaby, *Experiencing God Day-by-Day: The Devotional and Journal* (© 1997 by Broadman and Holman Publishers, Nashville, Tennessee). Reprinted and used by permission. ☩

Did You Know? Some Bible scholars and theologians affirm that the fourth person walking in the furnace was indeed Jesus Christ Himself. Such rare appearances are called *Christophanies*. Because Jesus is God and always was (John 1), it is possible that He appeared thousands of years before He was even born on the earth!

Today's Prayer: *Dear God, thank You for giving me the Holy Spirit to empower me, encourage me, and lead me in this life. Help me to yield to His power.*

Journal Question: Are you trying to resist temptation in your own strength or are you allowing the Holy Spirit to empower you?

_____

_____

_____

_____

_____

_____

_____

_____

_____

_____

_____

What does it mean to be a man or woman of grace?

Today's Teen: Esther
Today's Action Verse: Esther 2:17
Storyline: Esther 2:1–18

Esther Speaks Today: *"There is no limit to the impact of a man or woman guided by grace."*

Digging Deeper: Esther was born with rare beauty that helped her win the affections of the king of Persia. But more important than Esther's physical appearance was her personality. She was a young woman of grace and charm. These attributes not only won her a lot of friends and admirers but they also put her in a position to save her people from destruction.

Esther was a Jewish woman in a nation that hated Jews. She'd hidden her identity, but she had to reveal who she really was to save the Jewish people from being destroyed by a power-hungry bigot named Haman. Esther convinced King Ahasuerus (a.k.a. Xerxes, according to some Bible translations) to put a stop to Haman's racist plot (Esther 3–7).

God gives each person unique gifts. The gifts could be good looks, athletic abilities, a beautiful voice, a brilliant mind, or any number of other blessings. He's gifted you, like He did Esther, for a purpose. If you keep your gifts to yourself, then you probably won't help too many people in this world. But if you yield your gifts to the Creator, their Source, He'll help you fulfill your God-ordained destiny.

Just Like You: Sarah Bragg, author of *Body. Beauty. Boys.,* shares this thought about true beauty:

> What makes us yearn to be beautiful? Why is beauty the deep desire of every woman's heart? Some of us feel as though we would have a better life if we were more beautiful. Somehow we have believed the lie that beauty is everything. The Bible talks about beauty. It's not bad. Beauty becomes bad when it becomes the driving force behind what you do and why you do it. There are many women in the Bible who were known for their looks, but it was their inner beauty that played the most important role in their lives.
>
> Your outer beauty does not define who you are; we were misled into a false view of beauty. When you base your self-worth on a false view of beauty, you are bound to lose.
>
> Psalm 139:15 [NIV] says that your *"frame was not hidden"* from Him. Your frame is your body. Why do people go to art galleries? Do they look at the frames or the art inside those frames? No one goes to a gallery and stands in front of a painting and says, "Wow! Look at that frame. It is absolutely breathtaking!" We desire for our frame to be the attention grabber. God is more concerned with our artwork, our character. That is our real beauty.
>
> Our culture has given us an *unreachable* standard to attain. As Christians, we are not to live according to the world's standard. First Samuel 16:7 says, *"God sees not as man sees, for man looks at the outward appearance, but the Lord looks at the heart"* [NASB]. Our beauty and worth are established by God Almighty, the Creator of heaven and earth.
>
> —Sarah Bragg, author and conference speaker ✟
>
> (Visit Sarah's Web site at www.sarahbragg.com.)

Did You Know? Esther's original Hebrew name was *Hadassah,* which means "myrtle," a sweet-smelling floral shrub that produces berries. Esther, having been through a purification period with *"sweet odors"* (Esther 2:12), must have been very sweet smelling for her first visit with the king.

Today's Prayer: *Dear Lord, help me to be a person of grace who uses my gifts to influence others for Your glory.*

Journal Question: Are you measuring your worth by what others think of your outward appearance, or have you cultivated inner character? Write about your inner character.

_____

_____

_____

_____

_____

_____

✛ ✛ ✛ ✛ ✛ ✛ ✛ ✛ ✛   ✛ ✛ ✛ ✛ ✛ ✛ ✛ ✛ ✛

How can I use my influence to help someone in need?

Today's Teen: Esther
Today's Action Verse: Esther 4:14
Storyline: Esther 4–6

Esther Speaks Today: _"You'll be surprised how God can use you to make a difference for someone in need."_

✛ ✛ ✛ ✛ ✛ ✛ ✛ ✛ ✛ ✛ ✛ ✛ ✛ ✛ ✛ ✛ ✛ ✛ ✛ ✛

Digging Deeper: Brought up in a culture that despised Jewish people, young Esther changed her name and hid her Jewish identity. But God didn't forget her and had clearly put her in that situation for a purpose, which was to save the

Jews in that land from genocide. God had given her rare beauty, and He also gave her favor with the king. This young Jewish girl became queen of Persia. But that's not the end of the story. God had plans for Esther, plans to use her beauty, power, and influence to save the lives of many of His chosen people.

Prompted by Mordecai, Esther made the bold and life-threatening step of approaching her husband, the powerful and temperamental King Ahasuerus (a.k.a. King Xerxes) on behalf of her people. With courage, she said, *"If I die, I die"* (Esther 4:16 *The Message*).

God has put you where you are for a purpose, as He did Esther. There are no accidents and no coincidences in God's will. The circumstances of your life, which you cannot control, have been arranged and orchestrated by an all-powerful God.

Maybe you've kept your faith undercover, afraid of what you might lose if you step out. But there are people you can influence, lives you can shape, eternal destinies you can help change. Is it time for you to make a bold move for God?

Just Like You: How can you use your influence for God's glory? Ask yourself these questions:

- Can I share Christ with someone who respects me enough to listen?
- Is a friend of mine under attack? Can I defend that friend?
- What cause can I be a part of?
- Does my home, church, community, or school have a pressing need I can meet?
- Does a person in my realm of influence need some spiritual support and encouragement?
- Is there anything I can do to avert or prevent a potential disaster at school or home?
- Am I avoiding the addressing of a potential problem because I don't want to be criticized?

Did You Know? God's name is never mentioned in the book of Esther, but His divine hand is obviously present in the saving of the Jewish people from extermination.

Today's Prayer: *Dear God, I may not be queen or king of a country, but I know I can use my influence to help others, as Esther did. Help me to seize the opportunities before me and impact my generation for You.*

Journal Question: How can you be an Esther—a person of positive impact—in your church, school, family, or neighborhood?

_____

_____

_____

_____

_____

_____

✛ ✛ ✛ ✛ ✛ ✛ ✛ ✛ **DAY 96** ✛ ✛ ✛ ✛ ✛ ✛ ✛ ✛

When God comes looking for me, will I be ready?

Today's Teen: Mary
Today's Action Verse: Luke 1:28
Storyline: Luke 1:26–38

Mary Speaks Today: *"Be ready for God's call upon your life."*

✛ ✛ ✛ ✛ ✛ ✛ ✛ ✛ ✛ ✛ ✛ ✛ ✛ ✛ ✛ ✛ ✛ ✛ ✛

Digging Deeper: Before she became the famous mother of Jesus, Mary was just a quiet, God-fearing young lady who went about her business with grace and distinction.

God saw in Mary something special. Of all young women on the earth whom God *could have called* to carry out this special mission, Mary is the one God chose. Mary stood out from the others not for her outward appearance but for her inward spirit. She loved God with all her heart and served Him with sincerity. The job of raising the Son of God could not go to someone who was irresponsible or uncaring. Mary was responsible, spiritual, and *willing.* She had all the traits that made her the prime candidate for this special mission.

It doesn't necessarily matter to God what town you're from, who your parents are, or even if you're popular in school. All that matters is that you have a heart for God, a willing spirit, and a commitment to responsibility and faithfulness. These traits will make you a prime candidate to carry out God's calling upon your life.

Just Like You: Elizabeth George, in her book, *The Remarkable Women of the Bible,* says this about God's choice of Mary:

> Think about it. Think about the kind of woman God chose to be the mother of His only Son. Mary was *young*—unseasoned, inexperienced, unaccomplished, and unmarried. She had never been a mother. Mary was *poor*—possessing no fortune, no wealth, and no family inheritance. Mary was *unknown*—boasting no fame or social status. No one had ever heard of her father or mother—or her. Furthermore, nothing is said about her physical appearance or beauty. Clearly no one would choose Mary to be the mother of God's Son...except God! Despite what she lacked in the world's eyes, God sent His angel Gabriel to this poor, humble teenage girl....
>
> When the Lord went looking for a woman to bless as mother to His Son, He searched for a woman who loved God.
> —Elizabeth George, *The Remarkable Women of the Bible*

Do any of these characteristics describe you?

Did You Know? The choice of Mary fulfilled several Old Testament prophecies delivered hundreds of years before Christ's birth. She was a virgin (Isaiah 7:14), she was a descendant of David (Jeremiah 23:5; Psalm 132:11), and she was from the tribe of Judah (Genesis 49:10) (*Easton's Bible Dictionary*).

Today's Prayer: *Dear God, I want to be a servant in Your hands. I want to passionately pursue You with my whole being.*

Journal Question: Would you be ready if God called you for a special assignment? Why or why not?

_____

_____

_____

_____

_____

✛ ✛ ✛ ✛ ✛ ✛ ✛ ✛ ✛  ✛ ✛ ✛ ✛ ✛ ✛ ✛ ✛ ✛

Am I willing to be shamed for God?

Today's Teen: Mary
Today's Action Verse: Luke 1:28
Storyline: Luke 1:26–38

Mary Speaks Today: *"If God puts you in an uncomfortable position, He'll give you the grace to complete your mission."*

✛ ✛ ✛ ✛ ✛ ✛ ✛ ✛ ✛ ✛ ✛ ✛ ✛ ✛ ✛ ✛ ✛ ✛ ✛

Digging Deeper: Imagine Mary's disclosure to Joseph: "I'm pregnant. Oh, and did you know, it's the Son of God I am carrying?" Think of the awe that must have overtaken her and the questions that may have played on her mind: *What will Joseph think? What will my parents think? What will people think?*

God's call on Mary's life put her in a most uncomfortable position. She was pregnant and unmarried. And if it's hard for unwed mothers to make it today, it was many times harder back then. There were no churches or support groups to help carry the load. More than likely, the family wasn't exactly willing to welcome this baby with open arms. They probably shunned Mary. This was customary in that society.

But Mary soldiered on because she knew that this was God's will, God's promise to His people. She understood her special mission.

Maybe you're like Mary—thrust into an uncomfortable position because of your faith. Perhaps you feel out of place with society and out of place in your home, school, or neighborhood. Take comfort in Mary's life.

Just Like You: When BJ was young, his parents got divorced. Part of the time, BJ and his sister, Elsie, live with their dad, who takes them to church and tries to raise them in the Lord. But from Sunday through Wednesday, they have to stay with their mom and her new husband. BJ gets tired of shuffling back and forth from parent to parent. He wonders if and when he'll ever have a permanent place he can call home.

BJ wants to serve the Lord, but he often wonders why God has allowed him to be in such a touchy position. His mom questions his commitment to church and the ministry. Every night he wrestles with what is right.

BJ takes comfort in the story of Mary and in God's promise that all things will work together for his good (Romans 8:28).

Did You Know? Joseph and Mary were betrothed—kind of like being engaged. This usually happened an entire year before the marriage ceremony. Once a bride was betrothed to a groom, she was considered his wife even though the marriage didn't actually occur until at least a year later.

Today's Prayer: *Dear God, give me the strength and courage to follow You, even in uncomfortable situations.*

Journal Question: Would you be willing to be shamed for God as Mary was? Why or why not?

_____

_____

_____

_____

_____

✛ ✛ ✛ ✛ ✛ ✛ ✛ ✛ ✛ ✛ **DAY 98** ✛ ✛ ✛ ✛ ✛ ✛ ✛ ✛ ✛

Does God's grace extend to unwed mothers?

Today's Teen: Mary
Today's Action Verse: Luke 1:28
Storyline: Luke 1:26–38

Mary Speaks Today: *"God cares for those whom the world has left behind. He cares for the unwed mother struggling to raise her child in faith."*

✛ ✛

Digging Deeper: Ever since God promised Israel a Messiah, many Jewish women have dreamed of being the mother chosen for this special task. For centuries, Jewish women have wondered if their little boy would grow up to be the Messiah.

Don't you find it incredible that, of all the people in the world, God chose Mary, from an obscure family in a small town, to be the bearer of the Messiah? One of the reasons Mary was chosen was because she was a virgin, which was required for the fulfillment of God's miraculous, prophetic plan. But God's choice of Mary also reveals the grace of God. God cares about those whom society seems to have tossed aside—people like Mary, unknown and poor. In an instant, Mary's life changed: she became pregnant, though unwed—not an easy life.

You may be like Mary in one way—pregnant and unmarried. But unlike Mary, your dilemma may be the result of poor choices. That doesn't mean God loves you any less than He loves those who've done everything right. You may feel as though God has forgotten you because of your mistakes, but God cares about unwed mothers just as much as He cares about anyone else. He loves you and still has a plan for your life.

So if you're down about your condition, look to Mary for inspiration, because she, the most famous woman in history, was, at one time, pregnant and unmarried.

Just Like You: Amy grew up in a Christian home but ran away from home at the age of 15, turning her back on everything she was taught. She pursued a life of parties, drugs, alcohol, and relationships with men. At the age of 17, life hit bottom for Amy: She had no money, was living in the basement of a friend's home, and was pregnant.

As Amy pondered her future, she kept recalling the words her mom used to repeat over and over: *God loves you, Amy, and will always forgive you. You can always return to God. He's waiting with open arms.*

Amy knew that the tiny life inside of her may have been the result of poor choices, but it wasn't an accident. Yet she felt scared, used, and worthless. If she did come back, what kind of Christian could she be? Who would be her friend? Would her church even welcome her back? She had to at least try.

Desperate and broken, Amy called her mother and told her what had happened. She begged forgiveness for everything she'd done and told her mom that she wanted to start making the right choices. Would the family help her?

Fast-forward several years. Amy's first child is a five-year-old boy. He has a brother and a sister and a father. Amy is not only a married mother and wife but also a very active volunteer at her church. She says, "I realized that God doesn't love just those who have perfect families and who've made all the right choices. God also loves people like me who've made a mess of their lives. He wants to put our brokenness back together."

Did You Know? Mary was a virgin when she gave birth to Jesus, but she and Joseph went on to have more children. Among Jesus's brothers was James, who not only wrote a book of the Bible but also was the pastor of the very first church at Jerusalem.

Today's Prayer: *Dear God, thank You for Your grace, extended to me in spite of who I am. I know I am loved by You unconditionally. Help me to extend that same love and grace to those around me whose lives may not be perfect.*

Journal Question: How can God use you in spite of your mistakes? How can He use you to show His grace to others who have made mistakes?

_____

_____

_____

_____

_____

_____

_____

_____

_____

_____

_____

_____

_____

_____

_____

_____

Am I a pawn for someone else's evil desires?

Today's Teen: Salome
Today's Action Verses: Matthew 14:7–9
Storyline: Matthew 14:1–12

Salome Speaks Today: *"Don't allow yourself to be misused or abused by anyone. Don't be anyone's pawn. Rather, let your heart be directed by God."*

Digging Deeper: There is more to this bizarre and tragic story than meets the eyes. Behind the veil was a powerful, wicked woman, Herodias, who wanted to get revenge on John the Baptist, a godly man sent by God to preach the truth. John was a man with the courage to speak boldly.

The greatest tragedy is what happened to Salome, the teenage daughter of Herodias. Salome was subject to the whims of her evil mother. Together, they hatched a plot to seduce the king and extract from him what the mother wanted—John the Baptist's head. Salome's first mistake was allowing herself to be used as a cheap thrill—entertainment for a bunch of men. The second mistake was allowing herself to be a pawn in her mom's high-stakes chess match. Salome could have had anything in the kingdom, but she chose to go with her mother's evil desire—the death of one of God's greatest heroes.

Satan is like the evil, controlling mother, Herodias. He wants to use you as his pawn in his high-stakes battle against God. Be careful of his methods. He will come innocently disguised and whisper hollow promises. He will urge you to compromise your values. But ultimately, he seeks your destruction. Don't let the devil or people use you for their own gain. Stand up for yourself. Stand up for God's will and way for you.

Just Like You: In his book *Standing Tall,* James Scudder shares about Salome and the results of lack of courage, such as she displayed:

> Of all the things in the world, this young girl had no desire for the head of John the Baptist. Yet, she chose this over anything else in the kingdom. Why? She couldn't say no. She couldn't withstand the pressure.
>
> We head down the road of destruction when we don't have the courage to say no. Somewhere down the line, a powerful personality, acceptance in a peer group, or a supposed friend convinces us to fudge on our value system. For this woman, the powerful personality was her mother, Herodias. Charles Spurgeon said this: "Learn to say, 'No,' and it will be of more use to you than to be able to read Latin."
>
> This girl had no self-worth. She lived off the opinions of others. She danced to the delight of the Herodian men, selling her body for their pleasure. Her sense of purpose came only from satisfying the base appetites of those around her.
>
> It is easy to get our sense of self-worth from the wrong places. Hollywood tells us that sex appeal is everything. Madison Avenue convinces us that we have to have the right clothing. Our peer groups tell us that "everybody" is doing it. Even our family may smirk at our old-fashioned ways.
>
> Like this girl, we are fooled into believing that others' opinions are the benchmark of success. We do whatever it takes to garner that praise.
> —James A. Scudder, *Standing Tall* ✝

Did You Know? Herod's birthday celebration was no ordinary party. Because he was the ruler of Galilee and was known to enjoy lavish feasts, we can assume no expense was spared for this vain man's celebration.

Today's Prayer: *God, please give me the wisdom and courage to stand up and not allow myself to be used by someone else for his or her own base pleasure or personal gain.*

_____

_____

_____

_____

_____

✜ · ✜ ✜ ✜ ✜ ✜ ✜ ✜ · ✜   ✜ · ✜ ✜ ✜ ✜ ✜ ✜ ✜ ·

What if I don't have a lot to offer Jesus?

Today's Teen: Lunch Boy
Today's Action Verse: John 6:9
Storyline: John 6:1–14

Lunch Boy Speaks Today: *"God can turn your little into lots; He can make your limited means limitless in blessing others."*

✜ · ✜ ✜ ✜ ✜ ✜ ✜ ✜ ✜ ✜ ✜ ✜ ✜ ✜ ✜ ✜ · ✜ ✜ ✜ ✜ ✜ ✜ ✜ ·

Digging Deeper: Did you ever have an idea and share it, only to see it shot down by your friends or even your teachers or parents? Maybe it sounded good to you, but everyone else thought you were so dumb.

You can imagine, then, how this nameless young guy felt when he brought his lunch to Jesus. I picture him this way: stepping forth eagerly to offer his soggy peanut-butter sandwich, can of soda, bag of chips, and a few crushed cookies. Can you imagine Peter and the rest of the disciples rolling their eyes and thinking, *OK, so this guy thinks we can feed thousands of people with his sack lunch?*

But it was the young guy with the lunch who was the smartest person in the group. He offered what he had and left the results to Jesus. Jesus made this boy's pathetic little lunch feed that multitude of hot, hungry people.

Today Jesus is waiting for you to bring what little you have to Him. He wants to take your meager talents, gifts, and time and stretch them so your life can have an impact on more people than you ever thought possible.

Doubters will say that you're crazy for trusting God and that your faith is misplaced and outrageous. Don't worry about them. You'll have the satisfaction when Jesus does something seemingly impossible with your life.

Just Like You: God wants to do big things with your life, so be open to doing the "impossible."

- **Share your faith with a friend.** Maybe this person seems totally unlikely to come to church or youth group, but if you ask God for strength and the right moment to talk to him or her, God is likely to prepare that person's heart for your invitation. You never know what the response will be.
- **Be a leader in your school.** Maybe you're shy and you really don't want to create waves, but God can use you to influence other people to do the right thing, not necessarily by what you say, but by your life, your presence, and your actions.
- **Raise money for a cause in which you believe.** What can a few teenagers do? Maybe you and your friends can raise enough money to support a missionary or contribute to your church's building fund. Maybe you know of a poor family who needs a new car or improvements to their house. If you put your heads together and trust God for wisdom, you might be surprised by what He will do.

Did You Know? When John shared the story of this miraculous feeding of a multitude, he only mentioned how many men were present—5,000.

Matthew states in his account (Matthew 14:15–21) that women and children were also present. So the total number of people could have been as many as 20,000, enough to fill Madison Square Garden in New York.

Today's Prayer: *I know You want to do great things through me, so help me to surrender my gifts and talents to You for Your service. Stretch me and make my life have an impact on this world.*

Journal Question: In what ways can God stretch you? Why do you need to be stretched?

_____

_____

_____

_____

_____

_____

_____

_____

_____

_____

_____

_____

_____

_____

_____

_____

_____

Appendix B

✛ ✛ ✛ ✛ ✛ ✛ ✛ ✛ ✛ ✛ ✛ ✛ ✛ ✛ ✛

Suggested Resources

Helpful Magazines

- *Brio* (for girls) from Focus on the Family
- *Breakaway* (for guys) from Focus on the Family
- *YouthWalk* devotional magazine from Walk Thru the Bible
- *Ignite Your Faith* teen magazine from ChristianityToday.com

Helpful Web Sites or Blogs

- The Rebelution 1 Timothy 4:12 by Alex and Brett Harris (www.therebelution.com)
- Daretobelieve by teen author T. Suzanne Eller (www.daretobelieve.org)
- Devozine, teen devotionals, by The Upper Room (devozine.com)
- The One Year Bible Online (oneyearbibleonline.com)
- The Bible Gateway (www.biblegateway.com)
- Crosswalk's Bible Study Tools (biblestudytools.net)
- Search God's Word (www.searchgodsword.org)

Helpful Books

For Girls

- *Body. Beauty. Boys.* by Sarah Bragg
- *A Young Woman's Walk with God* by Elizabeth George
- *A Young Woman's Call to Prayer* by Elizabeth George
- *A Young Woman After God's Own Heart* by Elizabeth George

For Guys

- *A Young Man After God's Own Heart* by Jim George
- *Disciplines of a Godly Man* by R. Kent Hughes
- *Victory: The Principles of Championship Living* by A. C. Green
- *Thoughts for Young Men* by John Charles Ryle

For Both Girls and Guys

- *Growing Up Christian* by Karl Graustein
- *I Kissed Dating Goodbye* by Joshua Harris
- *Boy Meets Girl* by Joshua Harris
- *Not Even a Hint* by Joshua Harris
- *Passion and Purity* by Elisabeth Elliot
- *Beyond Failure* by James A. Scudder
- *The Purity Principle* by Randy Alcorn
- *Hudson Taylor's Spiritual Secret* by Howard and Geraldine Taylor
- *Changed into His Image* by Jim Berg

Selected Bibliography

Alcorn, Randy. *The Purity Principle: God's Safeguards for Life's Dangerous Trails.* Colorado Springs, CO: Multnomah, 2003.

Blackaby, Henry T., and Richard Blackaby. *Experiencing God Day-by-Day: The Devotional and Journal.* Nashville: Broadman and Holman, 1997.

Blunt, Sheryl Henderson. "The Unflappable Condi Rice." *Christianity Today,* September 2003.

Campbell, Donald K. *Daniel: God's Man in a Secular Society.* Grand Rapids, MI: Discovery House Publishers, 1988.

Elliot, Elisabeth. *Passion and Purity.* Grand Rapids, MI: Fleming H. Revell, 2002.

Ewald, Dan. "The Rebirth of Kirk Cameron." *Today's Christian,* March/April 2003.

Freeman, J. M., and Harold J. Chadwick. *The New Manners & Customs of the Bible.* Gainesville, FL: Bridge-Logos Publishers, 1998, 2004.

George, Elizabeth. *The Remarkable Women of the Bible.* Eugene, OR: Harvest House Publishers, 2003.

Harris, Alex, and Brett Harris. The Rebelution 1 Timothy 4:12 Web site. Available at: http://www.therebelution.com.

Harris, Joshua. *Not Even a Hint: Guarding Your Heart Against Lust.* Colorado Springs, CO: Multnomah, 2003.

Life Application Study Bible. Wheaton, IL: Tyndale House Publishers, 1989.

Pritchard, Ray. *Keep Believing.* Chicago: Moody Press, 1997.

Rainey, Dennis. *Parenting Today's Adolescent.* Nashville: Thomas Nelson Publishers, 1998.

Richards, L., and L. O. Richards. *The Teacher's Commentary.* Wheaton, IL: Victor Books, 1987.

Ryrie, Charles C., ed. *Ryrie Study Bible.* Chicago: Moody Publishers, 1994.

Smith, S., and J. Cornwall. *The Exhaustive Dictionary of Bible Names.* Orlando, FL: Bridge-Logos, 1998.

Stanley, Andy, and Stuart Hall. *The Seven Checkpoints for Youth Leaders.* West Monroe, LA: Howard Publishing, 2001.

Tan, P. L. *Encyclopedia of 7700 Illustrations.* Garland, TX: Bible Communications, 1979, 1996.

The Family Room, October 2004. Available at: www.FamilyLife.com/familyroom.

Towns, Elmer L. *How to Pray: When You Don't Know What to Say.* Ventura, CA: Regal Books, 2006.

Water, Mark, ed. *The New Encyclopedia of Christian Quotations.* Grand Rapids, MI: Baker Books, 2001.

Wiersbe, Warren W. *Be Decisive.* Be Series. Wheaton, IL: Victor Books, 1995, 1996.

Wiersbe, Warren W. *Be Obedient.* Be Series. Wheaton, IL: Victor Books, 1991, 1996.

Wiersbe, Warren W. *Wiersbe's Expository Outlines on the Old Testament.* Wheaton, IL: Victor Books, 1993.

Wilhelmi, Cheryl. "Saving Money, Saving Lives." Available at: http://www.briomag.com/briomagazine/reallife/a0007128.html.

Wilhelmi, Cheryl. "You Can't Put a Price on Life." Available at: http://www.breakawaymag.com/godfaith/a000000470.cfm.

Williams, Pat. *Who Wants to Be a Champion?* West Monroe, LA: Howard Publishing Co., 2005.

Willmington, Harold L. *Willmington's Book of Bible Lists.* Wheaton, IL: Tyndale House, 1987.

Wood, Gail. "Danny Wuerffel Finds Hope After Katrina." *Breakaway* 2005.

New Hope® Publishers is a division of WMU®,
an international organization that challenges Christian believers
to understand and be radically involved in God's mission.
For more information about WMU, go to www.wmu.com.
More information about New Hope books may be found
at www.newhopepublishers.com. New Hope books
may be purchased at your local bookstore.

Check these out ...

Radiant
*Discovering Beauty
from the Inside Out*
Chandra Peele
ISBN-10: 1-59669-089-5
ISBN-13: 978-1-59669-089-9

Priceless
*Discovering True Love, Beauty,
and Confidence*
Chandra Peele
ISBN-10: 1-56309-909-8
ISBN-13: 978-1-56309-909-0

Body. Beauty. Boys.
*The Truth About Girls and
How We See Ourselves*
Sarah Bragg
ISBN-10: 1-59669-008-9
ISBN-13: 978-1-59669-008-0

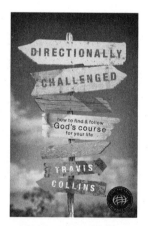

Directionally Challenged
*How to Find & Follow
God's Course for Your Life*
Travis Collins
ISBN-10: 1-59669-075-5
ISBN-13: 978-1-59669-075-2

Available in bookstores everywhere

For information about these books
or any New Hope product, visit
www.newhopepublishers.com.